Body.
Beauty.
Boys.

The Truth About Girls and How We See Ourselves

Sarah Bragg

new
hope
PUBLISHERS

Birmingham, Alabama

New Hope® Publishers
P. O. Box 12065
Birmingham, AL 35202-2065
www.newhopepublishers.com

Library of Congress Cataloging-in-Publication Data

Bragg, Sarah, 1978-
  Body, beauty, boys : the truth about girls and how we see ourselves / Sarah Bragg.
  p. cm.
  ISBN 1-59669-008-9 (softcover)
  1. Teenage girls—Religious life. 2. Body image in adolescence—Religious aspects—Christianity. I. Title.
  BV4551.3.B73 2006
  248.8'43—dc22
    2006000009

ISBN: 1-59669-008-9

N064134 • 0606 • 4.5M1

Body.

Beauty.

Boys.

Dedication

To my parents.

You have left a strong legacy in me to love God
and walk according to His truth.

To my husband.

Thank you for believing in me even when
I don't believe in myself.
I am exhilarated by your love.

TABLE OF CONTENTS

Foreword

Body image issues, eating disorders, and identity concerns are at the forefront of what girls struggle with today. The world is sending the messages that you can never be too thin and that everyone needs an "extreme makeover" to get their beauty to the "next level." Fortunately, God's Word tells us a different story. In this book, *Body. Beauty. Boys.*, Sarah Bragg brings a fresh voice to help girls learn about God's design—and it is much different from the world's.

Sarah reminds this generation of the promises of God and the fact that girls can rely on these promises to combat the lies of the world about how they should look, act, dress, and view themselves. She does a great job of taking stories from the Bible and weaving them throughout this book to illustrate and express the truth of God's view of what's important. This book is thoroughly grounded in Scripture. It's also presented in an interesting way so girls will "get it"—I know my 17-year-old daughter did.

Sarah came by her knowledge the hard way. She struggled with her own body image problem for years, and when God delivered her, He gave her a ministry. Sarah has worked in youth ministry for many years. She has seen many girls struggle with eating disorders and body image issues similar to hers, and seeing them triggered in her a desire to reach girls with God's truth. She has been through the journey, and girls will relate to, understand, and appreciate her personal insights and life experiences.

As girls read this book, they will find echoes of their own thoughts, fears, dreams, and desires. They will also learn that God wants something more for them than what the world can offer. Sarah cares enough to offer young ladies practical action steps to help them pursue God's dream. She carefully lays out the road map God provided her, and it will help other girls to become the women God envisions them to be.

Having watched Sarah work with girls during her time at Saddleback Church, I know that she has a message that resonates with this generation. Hers is a voice that girls listen to and one that I hope we hear more of in the future. I am honored to write the foreword for this book and will be eagerly awaiting stories of changed lives and fulfilled dreams that will come as a result of girls reading *Body. Beauty. Boys*.

Doug Fields
Pastor to Students: Saddleback Church
Author: *Purpose Driven Youth Ministry*
President: SimplyYouthMinistry.com

Introduction

The words from the Miss America song rang over and over in my head. I can remember singing them in the shower while I was growing up or humming as I sang them in my head while I played with my dolls. I knew only the first line to the Miss America song. I would just sing it over and over while I practiced my walk and wave. When at last I read the rest of the lines to the song, I was surprised at the very real pressure that goes with being Miss America. She will be the ideal and envy of millions of girls. I still sometimes sing the song to make my closest friend feel special when she walks through the door.

As a child, I was utterly fascinated with the Miss America Pageant. Even my favorite Barbie was Miss America. She won every year! I've wondered if all girls had that kind of fascination. I just knew I had been purposed even before the creation of the world to become Miss America.

Miss America is captivating, and the word captivating means "to attract and hold somebody's attention by charm or other pleasing or irresistible features." I think every woman on some level wants to be captivating. It's a normal desire that most girls have. Unfortunately, that desire can drive a person to obsession.

I wanted to be Miss America, and not just because I thought I was beautiful enough to win the pageant. The truth is I wanted to win in order to gain affirmation that I was beautiful on a national level. I wanted to be captivating. I thought that if I won, then maybe I could finally stop my obsession with my body, because I would have been recognized by all of America as being beautiful. At the time, I thought that was the only way for me to end my obsession with beauty. However, paying endless attention to the pageant did exactly the opposite of ending my obsession; it fed my obsession with my body. To be even more open with you, I will tell you that I also wanted every guy who had turned up his nose at me to regret the day he didn't ask me out on a date. I thought all those guys would kick themselves when they realized they could have dated the future Miss America.

My battle with body image lasted for a decade—from my childhood through college. Even today, I have moments of intense struggle. But I have found freedom in Christ, and so can you by making choices every day to believe truth rather than to believe lies. Through the truths and experiences presented in this book, I hope to help you find contentment with the way God has made you. I hope to paint a portrait of what freedom could look like in your life, if you believe God's truth.

Every Kind of Girl

God has given me the privilege of speaking to young women across the country and around the world. Some time back when I spoke at a girls' retreat in Orlando, Florida, I talked about my battle with body image. A middle-school girl came up to me after the message and said, "How could you have struggled with eating disorders? You are gorgeous!" Little did she know that even girls who look as though they have it all together may struggle with body image. Countless celebrities also battle with body image. I see their shrinking figures on the covers of magazines. It breaks my heart to see Lindsay Lohan, Hilary Duff, and Nicole Richie set the example of poor body image that girls try to imitate. I don't know what pressure they feel personally, but I do know the pressure that their physical appearances cause all of us who are watching. For girls and young women, there is an incredible amount of pressure to be beautiful.

If we have not yet found contentment in Christ, we tend to search and search for someone to make us feel good about ourselves. It's as if we walk up to every person we see or meet and ask that person to fill our cup to the top with compliments. "Please tell me I am pretty." "Please tell me I am worth something." "Please tell me that you will love me."

Instead of looking to other persons to fill our cup, we need to present our cup to God. Psalm 143:8 says, *"Let the morning bring me word of your unfailing love, for I have put my trust in you. Show me the way I should go, for to you I lift up my soul"* (NIV). When we seek God's *"unfailing love"* on a daily basis, we no longer feel the need to seek love and attention from others. God will fill our cup with His unfailing love, and then whatever we receive from others will just be an overflow.

To find freedom, we must first get to the heart of the matter—we must get to what's inside. We can try to cover up our hurt on the outside, but we will never be healed until we heal from the inside out. A quick-fix bandage on the outside will only last for a short time, but the results of internal healing will last forever. Freedom and healing come from God's truth, and that truth will set you free. This process takes time. It cannot be rushed.

When you begin to heal and change on the inside, your outside will begin to look different, too. I will always remember the time when a guy friend of mine complimented the way I looked as a result of my inner healing. He said, "I don't know what you have done differently, but it is as if you are glowing." I knew that what he had noticed was not the way I had fixed my hair that day or the new lip gloss I was wearing. I had finally found freedom because I had allowed God to change my inside, and it showed on the outside. Your outer beauty is only as striking as your inner beauty.

The purpose of this book is to put truth into your hands, and ultimately into your heart. God has given me a story to tell. It is a story about the lies I believed and then the truth that finally set me free. It's the story of one girl's struggle to find acceptance. It's a story that defines real beauty. It's a story that speaks to the heart of every woman. It's a story that breaks the illusion of beauty the world has so convincingly painted.

A Hidden Problem

Very few women, young or old, do not seek to make themselves more beautiful. Most women do not battle with clinically defined eating disorders, but I believe many women do struggle with a hidden obsession about food, exercise, and beauty. No one would look at me and think I would have struggled with my body image. No one would have considered my "healthy habits" to be troublesome. No one would have considered my exercising anything but wholesome. No one knew my exercise was excessive. It may be the same for you. You may seem confident. You may seem healthy. But for you, as for many women, deep down and hidden under the "healthy eating" and the "wholesome exercise" may lie a problem in your mind—a belief in untruths that cause you to define yourself according to the wrong standard of beauty.

Many young women have it all wrong. They seek desperately to find acceptance and completion from the wrong source. They say, "If only

I had a better body, then…" and "If only I had a boyfriend, then…." They fight a battle that they always seem to be losing. They compare themselves with the wrong standard. They raise themselves up against the world's standard.

To a young girl, Barbie is the ideal. She is perfect. I mean, she always gets the guy, and Ken is more handsome than all the others. As you have grown up, you have probably perceived that the grown-up world often works this way, too. In this book, I want to share how you can survive in a Barbie world. More than likely, you are reading this book because either you have a loved one who struggles with body image or you yourself struggle with it. I am not an expert on this subject. I am just a girl who suffered from a poor body image for more than a decade and is now free. Right now, I wish I could sit across from you while we sip our favorite coffee drinks and tell you my story. I want to help you recognize the lies of the world and show you how to replace them with the truth of God.

This is not a *self-help* book. This is a *God-help* book. This is a book that will point you to the only One who can truly help you. This is a book that will teach you to let go of self-control and allow the Sovereign God to take control. This is a book that will put truth in front of you. This is a book that is based on God's truth—what He says about you.

My prayer for you as you read this book is that you begin to see something about yourself that I couldn't see about myself for years. I pray that your mind will be freed so that you can see the real you, the way God sees you—beautiful.

CHAPTER ONE

How Does a Girl Survive in a Barbie World?

When I was a little girl, I had innumerable Barbie dolls. I had her town-home, Corvette, and even her family wagon. I once created a shopping center out of cardboard for my Barbie. I think that what I loved most about playing with Barbie dolls was that I could assign to them the identity of someone else by calling them the names of different celebrities. My dolls had the most amazing imaginary lives.

The Barbie Ideal

It's interesting that as I think back to my Barbie days, I don't recall her ever going on a diet or worrying about her self-image. Why do you suppose that was? Why did Barbie never diet? Why did it never occur to me that she might need to diet? It must have been because she was perfect and had a perfect life. She got everything she wanted—boyfriends, jobs, and clothes that fit perfectly. Years later, Mattel created the heftier Rosie O'Donnell doll to be Barbie's friend. But I didn't want that doll. I wanted the "normal-sized" Barbie. I wanted my perfect Barbie. I liked her skinny. Why did I think that way? Because in my mind, I, too, wanted to be perfect like Barbie. I always pretended to be her. She was my standard.

Many girls are like me. They have spent their lives trying to mold themselves into a perfect image like Barbie. Sometimes I wonder what it would have been like to grow up unaware of my body. What would it have been like to never ask: "Do I look good?" "Have I gained weight?" "Am

I pretty?" Barbie never thought about her weight. Barbie never compared herself with Skipper.

I want to pose a question for you to ponder: How does a girl survive in a Barbie world? I'm not going to answer that question just yet, but over the next few chapters I will help you understand how to survive in a beauty-obsessed culture and a world that holds before you to an unattainable standard.

Sticks and Stones May Break My Bones...

You, no doubt, recognize this familiar statement: Sticks and stones may break my bones, but words will never hurt me. I remember yelling those words at my older brother when he was antagonizing me. He would say something mean, and I would yell back, "Sticks and stones may break my bones, but words will never hurt me."

Where did I learn this declaration of independence? First of all, it's not a true statement. Sticks and stones may break my bones but words can break my heart and crush my spirit. Words have power—a power that can be used for good or for bad. Often, I don't think about the power I possess with my words. Matthew 12:36 says, *"But I tell you that every careless word that people speak, they shall give an accounting for it in the day of judgment."* To be careless means "to neglect or pay no attention." Many times I will speak careless words either to someone or about someone. I forget the power of words. I neglect to think about the other person's feelings.

I have also been on the other end of careless words, and they hurt me. They left scars—not physical scars, but hurtful scars on my heart and my mind. Those wounds left me feeling lonely and dead inside.

When I was ten years old, my family moved to Cleveland, Tennessee. We moved from a small town about 30 miles away, so it wasn't a big move, but enough to miss my friends and long for new ones. A girl at my school with whom I also went to church, invited me to her house for her birthday party. It was a pool party. I was excited about going to this party so that I could make some new friends. I was also nervous. The idea of a pool full of new people intimidated me.

Mom dropped me off at the house where the pool party was being held. I shut the car door and waved good-bye. Armed with a present in one hand and a swimsuit in the other, I headed down the path toward the front door. As I joined the party, I recognized many girls from my school and church. The girls were huddled together chatting. I entered the room and stood at the edge of those huddled girls. It's interesting that even though I am now 27 years old, I still have moments when I feel I'm standing at the edge of the huddled group. Some things just never change.

We walked out to the pool, but I still was not inside that group. The only friend I made that day at the pool party was a float—a float ring that fit around my waist and had an animal's head on the front. As I was playing with my new "friend," the float, something happened. I'm not sure how, but the float burst and deflated in my hands. I looked around to see if anyone was watching. I was so embarrassed that it had popped. In that moment, I heard something that was even more embarrassing. One of the girls from the group pointed and said, "Sarah's so fat she popped the float!" I was absolutely humiliated...totally crushed... devastated. I could not believe those awful words came out of that girl's mouth. I looked around and saw the other girls laughing, too. I tried to laugh with them, but couldn't. I tried to crack a smile; even that was hard. Could they tell I was utterly humiliated? Could they see the tears welling up in my eyes? In that moment, I realized for the very first time that I had an imperfect body.

> *Words have power—a power that can be used for good or for bad.*

The Beginning of Woes

From that moment on, I knew I never wanted to be in that situation again. Something had to be done. I determined I would never again be on the wrong end of criticism about my physical body, so I began dieting— at the age of ten! I took my lunch to school every day so that I would be sure to have a meal consistent with my diet. By the time I reached junior high school, the dieting had become obsessive. I watched what I ate like a hawk. I would not let myself exceed 1,200 calories a day. I carried a little spiral notebook with me everywhere to keep track of what I ate and how much I exercised. And it worked: I lost weight. I started getting compliments on my new figure, and I loved it. But I still wasn't satisfied. If the popular diet of the day didn't work, I would try something else. Either I wouldn't eat or I would binge and then throw up because I felt guilty for bingeing. I couldn't even eat something normal without feeling guilty.

Not only did I control my eating habits, but I also exercised relentlessly. Scared that I would lose my new shape because I had eaten too many cookies, I would exercise in the morning and then play tennis in the afternoon. I followed all this with a midnight run to burn off any excess calories I might have eaten during the evening. This behavior is called exercise bulimia. When you have this disorder, instead of forcing yourself to throw up after you eat, as happens in food bulimia, you force yourself to exercise because you ate something.

At this time in my life, I couldn't really see what I looked like. I would look in the mirror with disgust and think, "How could my body look this terrible?"

There was a void in me. I wanted to be noticed. I needed to be loved. I felt trapped and wanted to escape, but I couldn't. I wanted something, but didn't know what. Food was on my mind constantly. I thought about it when I woke up in the morning and during my classes, and it was the last thing I thought about when I laid my head on my pillow at night.

Between seventh and eighth grade, I lost 30 pounds. I went from a size 10 to a size 3. I looked like a completely different person than I did before I lost weight. Yet, the positive comments that I received still didn't quite satisfy me. They only fueled my obsession. With every year, my obsession grew; with every year, my dissatisfaction with myself grew; and with every year, the hole inside me got deeper and deeper. I felt trapped.

Subclinical Eating Disorders

I have a feeling that I am probably describing a lot of young women, most of whom have not been diagnosed with clinical eating disorder. In order for such a diagnosis to be made, certain side effects, such as loss of a menstrual cycle, must be experienced.

Most young women with thinking like mine do not have anorexia or bulimia, but suffer from lesser-known eating disorders. Girls with lesser-known eating disorders, since they cannot be clinically diagnosed as having an eating disorder, tend to believe they don't have a problem. But I still call obsessive thinking about eating and body image as I experienced a disorder, because that is what I believe it is. According to the dictionary, a disorder is "a medical condition involving a disturbance to the normal functioning of the mind or body." I got to the point I did not even know what was normal. My obsession seemed normal to me because it had been my mindset for so very long that I knew no other way to think. Two of the lesser-known disorders are anorexia athletica (compulsive exercising) and body dysmorphic disorder. A person who suffers from body dysmorphic disorder is obsessed with her looks. Instead of asking everyone if she looks fat, she will ask if she looks ugly. Many lesser-known body image disorders have been described, but I believe these two are the types most likely experienced by young women.

You might be reading this and wondering whether you have a problem. You, like many young women, may believe lies about your body. I remember reading information about eating disorders and being too afraid to see if the symptoms described me. I didn't want to have to admit that I had a problem. An unhealthy body image has some warning signs. Most of the following statements describe what I personally experienced. Do any of them ring true about you?

- ☐ I am critical of my body.
- ☐ I constantly think about what I am going to eat even if it is hours before a meal.
- ☐ I feel the need to exercise after I eat.
- ☐ I am always on a diet.
- ☐ I always think I could lose a few more pounds.
- ☐ I am scared to weigh myself because the number will plague me.
- ☐ When I get dressed, I wonder if others will think I look fat.
- ☐ I ask people to critique my appearance.
- ☐ I compare myself with other girls.
- ☐ I weigh myself often, and I am affected by the results.
- ☐ I choose what I eat based on what others eat.
- ☐ I am scared to eat in front of others, especially guys.
- ☐ I think that my life would be better if I were more beautiful.
- ☐ I find it hard to accept compliments from others.

I was never clinically diagnosed with an eating disorder, but the way I thought about my body was not normal. This obsession with my physical appearance was deeply guilt producing and self-defeating. I was hurting myself. I was incapable of loving myself, let alone loving someone else.

At this point, you may be squirming in your chair because I am describing you. You haven't felt normal in a long time. You feel trapped, and there's no place to go. How can you escape from something that is so consuming? I must tell you that you do not have to be consumed. Hope exists, and we will discover it together.

Causes of Eating Disorders

Eating disorders have many different causes. For me, **careless words** of another girl are what started me on the eating disorder path. Words can carry a mighty punch. I've never been in a physical fight before, but I can imagine how a fist to my face might feel. In addition to the immediate pain, it might leave a bruise that can be seen. Words bruise, too. The Bible says that words can either build up or tear down. Ephesians 4:29 says, *"Let no unwholesome word proceed from your mouth, but only such a word as is good for edification according to the need of the moment, so that it will give grace to those who hear."* Paul is the author of the book of Ephesians. The book is actually a letter written by Paul to a church in Ephesus.

It's interesting that Paul chose the word *"unwholesome"* to describe words that could proceed from our mouths. Unwholesome is the word

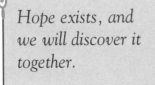

Hope exists, and we will discover it together.

used to describe something rotten. I cannot eat food that is close to its expiration date. I've been told that milk is OK to drink even up to a week after its expiration date, but I can't do it. It freaks me out. Once I opened a carton of milk after its expiration date, and I experienced the worst smell I had ever smelled. Consuming rotten food is like taking poison into your body. Our words can be rotten and poison us and hurt others when directed at them.

Paul then goes on to say that our words should be used for edification. He means that our words should build others up. I love compliments, and I know that you are the same way. Edifying, building-up words can make my day. Sometimes I wonder how my life would have been different if that girl at the pool party had chosen different words. What if she had chosen words that edified me? How would I be different? I think the sticks and stones saying should be revised to say, "Sticks and stones may break my bones, but *careless words can leave me lifeless.*" One girl's words sent me into a tailspin, and I ended up trapped because of the lies that I believed.

For some individuals, eating disorders are caused by the **pressure** they feel at home, at school, or in relationships. The pressure to perform can lead you to be extreme with your body. It can lead you to try to control something in your life, because everything else is being controlled by others. I have known many girls who have developed eating disorders because of pressure. They have unrealistic expectations put on them either by others or by themselves. I've seen girls get into dating relationships and then become obsessed with their bodies because they are afraid that if by chance they gain weight, the guy will be out the door. When I was in high school, someone told me that the way you get a guy is the way you will have to keep him. If you win him over by your appearance, then you will feel the pressure to keep him with your appearance. If he is only attracted to your body, then you will have to work hard at keeping your body perfect. On the other hand, if you attract him with something other than the physical, say your personality or spirit, then he was attracted to the real you. The pressure pushes you down a deadly spiral and, as with careless words, you are left lifeless.

According to ANRED (Anorexia Nervosa and Related Eating Disorders, Inc.) statistics, more than half of teenage girls are or think they should be on a diet. I rarely meet a girl who doesn't think she could or should lose a few pounds. The average woman is 5 feet 4 inches tall and weighs 145 pounds. Proportionately, Barbie is estimated to be an even 6 feet tall and 101 pounds. If she is our ideal, it is no wonder so many of us have a complex. We grow up being fascinated with a figure that no one can achieve.

The pressure to look good can lead to drastic measures. In order to fit into what the culture deems as fit, girls succumb to dieting. If dieting doesn't work, some turn to starving themselves or to bingeing, only to later throw up what they ate. In response to pressure, girls may develop an imbalance and do everything to the extreme. Starving yourself is not living in balance. Exercising three times a day is not living in balance. These things constitute drastic measures.

Resulting Loneliness and Discouragement

When you suffer from an obsession with your body, it leaves you feeling lonely and isolated. When that girl said that I was fat, I was the only one not laughing. I felt as though I was watching myself from afar. I felt totally alone at that moment. My obsession drove me to more loneliness. Embarrassed about my disorder, I didn't want to tell anyone about it, so I battled alone. I didn't invite anyone to help me, and no one prayed with or for me. I was all alone.

When you suffer from an eating disorder, you not only feel alone, but you also get discouraged. When you are displeased with yourself, nothing makes you happy. Every time you walk past a mirror, you inspect your appearance. You never leave a mirror encouraged by what you see. Every time you see another girl who is pretty, you compare yourself and become discouraged with the way you look. The discouragement feeds your eating disorder.

We cannot separate our emotions from our physical state. Think about premenstrual syndrome (PMS). I cannot think clearly when I have PMS. I adore my mother for three weeks of the month and then fight her on everything during that one week of PMS. During PMS, I always feel differently about my body. Someone might pay me a compliment, but because I have PMS, I will have a hard time believing the compliment. We let our feelings dictate what we believe. We feel lonely. We feel discouraged. Therefore, we see food and our bodies through the lens of an unhealthy obsession.

The Comparison Game

Over the course of my life, I have constantly been the guest star for the imaginary game show called *The Comparison Game*. I used to play it every day. This game began when I compared myself with celebrities. I was fascinated with the Hollywood stars. I wanted to know what they were wearing and whom they were dating. I watched all the entertainment shows and read all the gossip magazines. I would look at them and mentally size myself up by them. A few times, I actually felt like I stood a chance next to them.

My fascination with Hollywood seemed innocent, but I found that I was *constantly* comparing myself with the stars, and that was *not* so innocent—*not* so harmless. My comparison game went further than that, however. I was actually comparing myself with everyone I met, not just celebrities. I would ask myself comparison questions: "Do I look like her?" "Are my hips as big as hers?" "Am I prettier than she?" I reached the point at which I couldn't even see who I was or what I really looked like.

Body. Beauty. Boys.

After playing the comparison game for a while, I learned that when you compare yourself with others, you lose every time. You lose by either putting yourself down or by exalting yourself.

The Sin of It All

Comparing yourself with others may seem innocent, but it is actually sin. I had never looked at it this way until I read Galatians 1:10, which says, *"For am I now seeking the favor of men, or of God? Or am I striving to please men? If I were still trying to please men, I would not be a bond-servant of Christ."* In Greek, *"seeking the favor"* means "to seek to persuade or solicit or entice." Many times in my life, I sought to persuade people to focus on me.

Have you ever heard a scriptural passage a thousand times, but then you suddenly glean a new truth from it? Let me share a time that happened for me. While I want to be a humble person, I realize I do have a tendency toward pride, so one time I looked up some Scriptures that focus on pride. This following passage grabbed me:

> *You younger men [women], likewise, be subject to your elders; and all of you, clothe yourselves with humility toward one another, for God is opposed to the proud, but gives grace to the humble. Therefore humble yourselves under the mighty hand of God, that He may exalt you at the proper time, casting all your anxiety on Him, because He cares for you.*
> —1 Peter 5:5–7

The verses address humility and pride. Pride is self-absorption. Eating disorders are very prideful diseases, because they force us to focus on ourselves. You can understand why the passage grabbed me when I read *"God is opposed to the proud, but gives grace to the humble."*

When I was younger, I had no idea what it meant to humble myself. When I read this passage from 1 Peter 5, I could not understand why the admonition to humble yourself was followed by the instruction to cast all your anxieties on God. In reading this passage over and over, God spoke to me, and I *finally* understood: God wants us to clothe ourselves in humility toward everyone. We are also to humble ourselves under God, and He will exalt us in due time. *Therefore*, we need to cast our anxieties about our bodies on God, because He *will* exalt us in due time—His time—whether that be on earth or in heaven, or whether it is in front of others or alone. His attention outweighs the attention of others.

Consumed

I didn't date much in high school. I thought the reason was because I was ugly. Because of my belief, I came up with a plan. I decided I would enter beauty pageants. I wanted to be Junior Miss. I began preparing my piano solo and picking out dresses. Before registration even began, the pageant was canceled. It was the only year that it was ever canceled. Do you think it was coincidence, or did God have humbling motives behind what happened? However, a canceled pageant didn't stop me.

I then decided to try to become Miss America. If I succeeded no one could ever deny my beauty and talent. All those guys who didn't ask me out would regret the day they looked away from me. (I hope you're laughing at me right now, because I am.) Once again, God didn't open the door for me to enter this pageant either.

Then I realized that I was seeking the favor of men rather than the favor of God. Pride had crept into my life. The pressure to look good can lead to drastic measures. The Greek word in Galatians 1:10 for bond-servant is *doulos*, which means to be altogether *consumed* in the will of the other. I was altogether consumed by my own will because I was consumed with the way I looked. Are you altogether consumed by something? How can you be altogether consumed in yourself? Let me put it this way. Do you inspect yourself in front of every mirror? Do you constantly think about your body? Do you think about your lunch and dinner before you've even eaten breakfast? Do you eat something and then immediately feel the need to exercise? Do you always think about the calories in what you eat? Is every meal a battle of what to eat and what not to eat? I have realized that I want to be a servant of God, but I can't when I am consumed by my own will. God created us. Romans 11:36 says, *"For from Him and through Him and to Him are all things. To Him be the glory forever. Amen."* We are from Him, and we were created for Him. We need to be altogether *consumed by His will.*

Not only are we to be altogether consumed by His will, but the Bible also says that our ambition should be to walk in a manner worthy of the Lord to please Him.

For this reason also, since the day we heard of it, we have not ceased to pray for you and to ask that you may be filled with the knowledge of His will in all spiritual wisdom and understanding, so that you will walk in a manner worthy of the Lord, to please Him in all respects, bearing fruit in every good work and increasing in the knowledge of God.
—Colossians 1:9–10

Therefore we also have as our ambition, whether at home or absent, to be pleasing to Him.
—2 Corinthians 5:9

What does it mean to walk in a manner pleasing to the Lord? Our primary ambition should be *to please Him* rather than to please others or ourselves. When we compare ourselves with other women, what is our ambition? Is it to please others? Is it to please ourselves? Is it to please God? I don't believe that comparing ourselves with other women pleases God.

In the Bible, Abraham's wife Sarah compared herself with Hagar. She was jealous of Hagar because Hagar could bear children and she, Sarah, could not. Nowhere in this story does it say that Sarah's actions pleased God. (See Genesis 16.)

Comparing ourselves to others only leads to loss. The rule I have established for myself is this: *Go out of your way to celebrate publicly whatever threatens you privately.* I keep a magnet on my refrigerator that simply says the word *celebrate*. I am reminded every day to celebrate others. I don't mean that I actually throw a party for the person of whom I am jealous. To celebrate means to show happiness about something or someone. If you are jealous of someone, celebrate first with God whatever it is that threatens you, and then celebrate it with that person. The more you celebrate, the more jealousy will be weeded out of your heart. If you celebrate without reserve, your jealousy will be cured.

In Genesis, the first book in the Old Testament, two brothers are mentioned in a genealogy rundown. Sometimes it is easy to get lost in Scripture, especially when it starts talking about genealogy, but something really important can be found here, so bear with me through this. Genesis 4:17–20 lists descendants of Cain:

Cain lay with his wife, and she became pregnant and gave birth to Enoch. Cain was then building a city, and he named it after his son Enoch. To Enoch was born Irad, and Irad was the father of Mehujael, and Mehujael was the father of Methushael, and Methushael was the father of Lamech. Lamech married two women, one named Adah and the other Zillah. Adah gave birth to Jabal; he was the father of those who live in tents and raise livestock. His brother's name was Jubal; he was the father of all who play the harp and flute. Zillah also had a son, Tubal-Cain, who forged all kinds of tools out of bronze and iron.

—Genesis 4:17–22 (NIV)

Several of these men are remembered for careers or honors that were impressive. One built a city. One had a city named after him. One was known for his livestock. One was known for being a great musician. One was known for creating tools of bronze and iron. These activities and honors are impressive to people; thus, these men were thought of highly by other people. These five men were noted for lives that pleased or impressed others.

Then, the Bible lists the descendants of one of Cain's younger brothers, Seth. Seth had a great great great grandson who *also* was named Enoch. This Enoch was *not* remembered for anything that would normally impress others. In fact, we aren't even told what his career was. But in Genesis 5:22 and 24, we are told that *"Enoch walked with God"*—that is what he is remembered for. That simply means he lived a life in communion with God, a life that was pleasing to God. And that, ladies, is what it's all about. It's about being altogether consumed by what pleases God.

Do you know what pleases God? Having the right view of your body is one thing that surely pleases God. Not comparing yourself with every other girl you see is something else that pleases God. Right thinking about your body pleases God. Treating your body with respect is pleasing to our Lord God, because, after all, He has a purpose for your body.

Or do you not know that your body is a temple of the Holy Spirit who is in you, whom you have from God, and that you are not your own?

—1 Corinthians 6:19

Three Steps

As we begin this journey together, I want to challenge you to recognize three things: you may have a problem, you are not the only one who has suffered with this problem, and comparing yourself with others is a sin.

First of all, **recognize that there is a problem**. I know that it sounds something like a twelve-step program. That's okay. This is where we need to start. We will talk more about how we should view our bodies, but for now I just want you to recognize that a problem exists.

Next, **recognize that you are not the only one** who has suffered through a problem like this. You are not alone in this battle. Many women have suffered and still suffer from eating disorders of many kinds. Not only are there many people who can empathize with you, but there is One being who is with you always. God will never leave you or forsake you. He is the One who feels your pain. You are not fighting this battle alone. Choose to take your feelings to God. Choose to cast all your anxieties upon Him. Choose to cry out to Him. I promise that He will hear you.

> *When you compare yourself with others, you lose every time. You lose by either putting yourself down or by exalting yourself.*

Finally, **recognize that comparing yourself with others is a sin**. Simply call it what it is—sin. Constantly comparing yourself with other girls and feeling either better or worse about yourself because of the comparison you made are sin. Comparison causes you to miss the mark about God's intended purpose for your life. You never win when you play the comparison game. Some of us tend to think that pride is only exalting ourselves. But having a poor body image is also a prideful disease of the heart.

You might be saying: "But, Sarah, I *don't* think highly of myself. How can I be prideful?" Thinking too little of yourself is just as prideful as thinking too greatly of yourself. It's just the other extreme. Either way, you are being self-absorbed.

I want to challenge you not to compare yourself with anyone for the next few days. Whenever comparison thoughts enter your mind, turn away from them and thank God for the way He created you. Whenever you see a pretty girl, thank God for the way He created her. See what kind of difference it makes in your day when you don't compare yourself with others.

For many, many years, my body was the only thing on my mind. I was distracted around other people because I had to think about what I was eating at all times. It was absolutely exhausting. It occupied all my thoughts—all my time. "Sticks and stones may break my bones, but words will never hurt me." Oh, how I wish that were true, but it is the furthest thing from the truth. Words can pack a powerful punch that can leave you obsessed, lonely, and lifeless. As you turn the page to the next chapter, turn the page in your life, and open your heart to the hope that God wants to give you.

Bible Study Questions

1   Memorize 1 Peter 5:7. Write 1 Peter 5:5–7 on a card so that as you memorize verse 7, you will be reminded of why you should cast your anxieties on God.

2   What is your standard of beauty?

3   Read Matthew 12:36. Write down the names of persons who have offended you with their careless words.

4   Read Ephesians 4:29. Write down the names of those whom you have offended with your careless words.

5   Write down any of the statements on page 21 that you have found yourself thinking.

6   What kind of pressure to be beautiful do you feel? How is this a prideful condition? Reread 1 Peter 5:5–7.

7   Read Galatians 1:10. How is comparison a sin?

8   Can beauty be a sin? What is your ambition in beauty? Read 1 Peter 3:3–4.

Body. Beauty. Boys.

Write your reactions to Sarah's thoughts in this chapter. Which thoughts relate to you? Which ones don't relate to you? How did you feel as you read?

_____

_____

_____

_____

_____

_____

_____

_____

_____

_____

_____

_____

_____

_____

Blurred Vision

What makes us yearn to be beautiful? Why is beauty the deep desire of every woman's heart? Some of us feel as though we would have a better life if we were more beautiful. Somehow we have believed the lie that beauty is everything. The truth is that beauty isn't the most important quality to people around the world. The Bible talks about beauty. It's not bad. Beauty becomes bad when it becomes the driving force behind what you do and why you do it. There are many women in the Bible who were known for their looks, but it was their inner beauty that played the most important role in their lives. Your outer beauty does not define who you are, although the world tells you it does. It is your inner beauty that defines you.

Somewhere along the way, we were misled into a false view of beauty. When you base your self-worth on a false view of beauty, you are bound to lose. Throughout this chapter we are going to explore what beauty is and how, in our attempts to feel beautiful, we fall into different traps. Those traps are immodesty, impurity, and perfectionism.

My eyesight has been bad for as long as I can remember. I started wearing glasses in the second grade. My vision was so bad that if you were sitting a few feet in front of me I wouldn't be able to recognize you. In fact, I couldn't even read the clock that was beside my bed. Before junior high school, I wore big blue-rimmed glasses. I guess that was the style then, but looking back it's pretty embarrassing to think about how I looked. Next, I graduated to contacts; they, thankfully, were much more acceptable.

The amazing thing about corrective lenses is their ability to give sight. When I wake up in the morning, the first thing I do is put on my glasses or put in my contacts. Being able to see clearly gives me a whole new perspective on what my apartment looks like. As nearly blind as I am, I would be crazy to walk around the house without my glasses. I would run into furniture and stub my toes. And it would be absolutely crazy for me to leave the house without wearing some kind of vision correction.

Some of us need some vision correction to see what our bodies really look like. Some of us have had blurred vision for a very long time. In the first chapter, we pointed out some things that might indicate a problem exists. Now I want to dive a little deeper into the problem.

I have met people who have poor vision, but refuse to admit it. They try to cover up the fact they have poor vision by diverting attention to something else so that people won't pick up on the fact that they can't see. They don't want to read when called upon. They don't want to drive. The same thing happens when it comes to a poor body image. Not only have I seen it in others, but I've seen it in myself, too. I have tried to cover up the fact that I have blurred vision about my appearance. I want to talk about three cover-ups: immodesty, impurity, and perfectionism.

Immodesty

Many girls who suffer from a blurred vision of their body will dress immodestly to feel better about their appearance. I know this thinking. This cover-up says, "If I can show a little and get attention, then it means I have a nice body." So the shorts become shorter. The shirts become smaller. The clothes become tighter. We wear clothes that divert attention away from the real problem. We cover up what's going on inside our hearts. The problem in your heart might look different from the problem in my heart; so you might not see your specific problem described, but you may recognize some symptoms.

Everyone has a different definition or opinion of modesty. The world has a certain view of modesty. It's sad to say, but we often buy into the world's definitions to cover up our heart problem. The Bible has a certain view of modesty. It doesn't say to wear a garbage bag, but it does give us clear principles by which to live.

Immodesty is rooted in a false view of beauty. The world defines beauty as strictly outer appearance. Most beauty pageants judge girls on the way they look in swimwear and evening gowns. Their talent is often overlooked. In fact, the Miss America pageant has considered dismissing the talent round altogether.

I recently watched a television show on VH1 about celebrity beauty. The interviewers uncovered the pressure that celebrities feel to be beautiful. Celebrities admitted that the thinner they are, the more acceptance they find in Hollywood. The better their outward appearance, the better roles they receive. And let's face it—this isn't only true in Hollywood; it's true in my world and your world, too.

With our world screaming the wrong definition of beauty, how can anyone get the right view of beauty? Only the truth of God can overcome the lies that we have believed for so long. God's Word shows us how fleeting physical beauty is and how important inner beauty is. Proverbs 31:30 says, *"Charm is deceptive, and beauty is fleeting; but a woman who fears the LORD is to be praised"* (NIV). The New American Standard Bible translates the word *fleeting* as vain. Vanity means nothingness. It doesn't matter. It doesn't last. This verse gives the impression that you should not waste your time and efforts on something that is nothing. We put so much of our time and efforts into external beauty hoping it will satisfy a craving that in reality only God can satisfy.

The woman in Proverbs 31 was not praised for her beauty, but for her character. According to this verse, physical beauty is not praiseworthy, but the fear of the Lord is. The fear of the Lord is the awesome dread of displeasing Him. This would mean that in everything we do, we should have a holy reverence for Him and the goal of pleasing Him. We fear Him by our response to Him—worship, trust, obedience, and service.

The way you dress is a response to God. We need wisdom when it comes to determining whether an outfit is modest or not. The beginning of wisdom is recognizing that wisdom can only originate with God. Real intimacy with God comes out of our respect and reverence for Him—our awe of Him.

> *For great is the LORD and greatly to be praised;*
> *He is to be feared above all gods.*
> *For all the gods of the peoples are idols,*
> *But the LORD made the heavens.*
> *Splendor and majesty are before Him,*
> *Strength and beauty are in His sanctuary.*
> —Psalm 96:4–6

This awe allows us to be completely vulnerable before Him because He is our Creator and knows us fully.

Robert Nisbet wrote about the fear of God: "It is the fear which a child feels towards an honoured parent—a fear to offend.… Such is the fear of the Christian now: a fear which reverence for majesty, gratitude for mercies, dread of displeasure, desire of approval, and longing for the fellowship of heaven, inspire." (*The Songs of the Temple Pilgrims*, 1863)

I know exactly what this means. I love my father dearly, and I have always wanted to please him. To this day, I still won't wear a miniskirt or get my belly button pierced because I don't want to displease my father. I know he would hate it, so I show him respect by not doing it. Does that mean it is wrong to pierce my belly button? No, but I want to show my earthly father respect. I should have the same motivation to please my heavenly Father.

A big part of respecting God with our bodies has to do with our view of Him. Ecclesiastes 3 speaks of this:

> *I know that there is nothing better for them than to be glad and to get and do good as long as they live;*
> *And also that every man should eat and drink and enjoy the good of all his labor—it is the gift of God.*
> *I know that whatever God does, it endures forever; nothing can be added to it nor anything taken from it. And God does it so that men will [reverently] fear Him [revere and worship Him, knowing that He is].*
> —Ecclesiastes 3:12–14 (AMP)

Note that the *Amplified Bible* defines the fear of the Lord as "*to revere and worship Him, knowing that He is.*" You fear Him because you know that He is. You know His character. You know why He deserves and requires our worship and adoration. We need to respect Him in our adornment simply because of who He is and what He has done.

The book of 1 Peter addresses the issue of modesty.

> *Your beauty should not come from outward adornment, such as braided hair and the wearing of gold jewelry and fine clothes. Instead, it should be that of your inner self, the*

unfading beauty of a gentle and quiet spirit, which is of great
worth in God's sight.
—1 Peter 3:3–4 (NIV)

These verses do not teach that physical beauty is sinful. It is not wrong to pay attention to our outward appearance. The author of 1 Peter was not saying to ignore the outer adornment, but we also need to adorn ourselves with a heart that is beautiful. According to this verse, a beautiful heart is one that is holy.

Nowhere in Scripture is physical beauty condemned. What is condemned is taking pride in God-given beauty and giving excessive attention to physical beauty while ignoring matters of the heart. The heart is what is most important. What is on the inside is what will be seen on the outside. That's what I meant by saying the way you dress makes a statement about who you are. You are God's child. The way you dress says something about God. As Christian women, we should seek to reflect the beauty and grace of God through both our outward and our inner beauty.

The big story in the book of Esther is about Esther, so Queen Vashti, who was known for her beauty as discussed in the first chapter of that book, is often overlooked.

> *On the seventh day, when the heart of the king was merry*
> *with wine, he commanded…the seven eunuchs who served in*
> *the presence of King Ahasuerus, to bring Queen Vashti before*
> *the king with her royal crown in order to display her beauty to*
> *the people and the princes, for she was beautiful. But Queen*
> *Vashti refused to come at the king's command delivered by the*
> *eunuchs. Then the king became very angry and his wrath*
> *burned within him.*
> —Esther 1:10–12

Queen Vashti exuded inner confidence. The king wanted her to flaunt her beauty in front of a lot of drunken princes, but she refused. In spite of the fact that her refusal could have meant death, she stood for what she thought was right. She knew it wasn't appropriate to flaunt her outer beauty. It took a great deal of inner confidence to do what she did and to refuse the king. Inner confidence is beautiful.

I just watched the film *A Walk to Remember*. The main character, Jamie Sullivan, played by Mandy Moore, was definitely modest in the way she dressed. The heartthrob, Landon Carter, played by Shane West, fell for her, but not because of her outward appearance. He was attracted to the inner confidence that exuded from her. What this says is that the girl who is confident of who she is in Christ and who is confident in her inner beauty has no need to flaunt herself around guys.

Think about it. The girls who flaunt themselves appear to be the confident ones, but really the confident girls have no need to flaunt themselves because they are secure in who they are. A sure sign that you have blurred vision when it comes to beauty is that you act and dress in an immodest way. I exhort you to not cover up a lack of confidence about your body by being immodest; rather, as you grow in Christ, unveil what is really going on in your heart.

Impurity

Not only do we cover up with immodesty, but we also cover up with impurity. This was the cover up I adopted when I struggled with body image. I was so insecure with my outward appearance that I allowed impurity to creep into my life in order to feel better about my appearance. I allowed impurity to compensate for my blurred vision. Here's how.

I thought that if a guy was physical with me, then I must be attractive. No guy would want to be physical with a girl who was ugly. Therefore, I allowed myself to do things with guys that I had never imagined doing until marriage. Not every girl struggles with impurity because of a poor body image, but I believe a lot of girls do.

> *I thought that if a guy was physical with me, then I must be attractive.*

If we deal with what's really going on in our hearts by covering it up, we will never be able to receive healing. We often nurse the bigger need with something that isn't satisfying. Psalm 145:16 says of God, *"You open Your hand and satisfy the desire of every living thing."* We oftentimes try to satisfy a spiritual craving in physical ways. Whatever you desire, God will satisfy. I believe God will even satisfy your desire to be known as beautiful.

The truth came to me that I was physical in relationships because I wanted someone to tell me that I was hot and that he wanted my body.

I didn't have a healthy view of myself, and I didn't see myself through God's eyes. Some of you have spent your whole life wanting someone to choose you, approve you, and accept you. Some of you are going too far with a guy because you are longing to be chosen as beautiful. But it has already happened. God said you are beautiful. Psalm 45:11 says, *"Then the King will desire your beauty. Because He is your Lord, bow down to Him."* I want you to be empowered to remain pure and to believe that you do not need the affection of men to feel beautiful.

To help you avoid impurity in your dating relationships, you would be wise to determine your reason for dating, create a standard for the type of person you would consider dating, and establish boundaries up front.

Determine your reason for dating. If you want to protect your purity, first of all commit not to date until you have settled on just why it is you really want to date. What are you looking for by dating? Are you looking for acceptance? …affirmation of popularity or beauty? …intimacy? What is it that you really want? Sometimes I walk into my kitchen at home looking for something to eat. I walk back and forth between the refrigerator and the pantry. The problem is that I don't know what I want. I just want something—some certain thing—but I don't know what it is! We can be like that in our quest for dates. We go back and forth because we really don't know what we want. We want something specific, and we don't even know what!

So again I ask: What is it that you really want out of a dating relationship? You need to know the answer to that question before you begin dating. Otherwise, you might find yourself in the same trap into which I fell. As I have said, I dated to feel more beautiful. I reasoned that guys don't date unattractive girls, so if they dated me, then I must be attractive. I didn't understand a valuable principle. I didn't understand that you and I have intrinsic value. Intrinsic means "by or in itself, rather than because of its associations." You have value—worth— apart from externals. You have value—not because of your body, hair, or externals and not because of what is said about you—you have value because you were created by God in His image. Genesis 1:27 says, *"God created man in His own image, in the image of God He created him; male and female He created them."* Relationships go wrong when you forget that truth.

A lot of times, we get into relationships in order to feel valued. We wait for someone to give us value. We hold a cup up to every single person we meet, asking that person to fill us up with value. "Tell me I look pretty." "Tell me you want me." "Tell me you love me." "Tell me you want to date me." "Tell me you'll call me."

The truth is that we don't need these affirmations to have value. We already matter to God. *"God has chosen you from the beginning for salvation through sanctification by the Spirit and faith in the truth"* (2 Thessalonians 2:13). You are chosen. You are chosen through faith in Christ. We have intrinsic value in Christ. Whatever it is that we are looking for can be found in Him!

Create a standard for dating. After you have settled on why you want to date, and you determine that you are ready to date, create a standard for the men you date. Proverbs 4:23 says, *"Above all else, guard your heart, for it is the wellspring of life"* (NIV). The heart needs to be guarded because it is the seat of all affections. If you have a physical heart problem, it will affect everything about you. If you have a heart attack, it will not just hurt your heart, it will hurt your arm, your legs—your entire body. The same is true of our spiritual hearts; if we have a spiritual heart problem, it will affect our entire spiritual being. That's why we must guard our hearts.

After I graduated from high school, I did what I am suggesting you do. I guarded my heart by creating a standard for dating. My standard helped me rule out certain guys. This standard wasn't about a guy being tall, dark, and handsome; rather it was about character qualities. My standard included a list of 22 qualities. I combined all of those qualities into only three so that I could easily memorize them. Here is the standard for the guy I wanted:

- A guy who loves the Lord and is pursuing a relationship with Him
- A person to whom I am totally attracted
- One who makes me laugh so hard I can't stop

I wrote my standard on a note card that I kept in my Bible at Psalm 37:4. This verse says, *"Delight yourself in the LORD; and He will give you the desires of your heart."* I have read the standard over and over. You may be tempted to settle for less, but don't do it. Even though you may grow weary of dateless nights, in the long run, being with the right kind of guy will make it worth the wait.

I don't look back on my life and wish that I had dated more in high school. Proverbs 16:3 says, *"Commit to the LORD whatever you do, and your plans will succeed"* (NIV). Commit your standard for dating to the Lord, and you will succeed. (As I write these words, I find myself smiling. God's promise came true in my life. I was married during the writing of this book, and the Lord blessed me with a man who met every part of my standard.) God wants to bless you beyond expectations, and He will when you commit to honor Him with your selection criteria for whom you date.

Establish boundaries. Once you determine your reason for dating, create a standard for dating, and then actually begin dating, I want to encourage you to set boundaries and make them known. Boundaries are important. I used to think boundaries didn't matter, and I got into some compromising situations because I had no boundaries. I used to think I was strong enough to say no when I needed to do so. Many girls I meet ask me the same question: "How far is too far?" The Bible doesn't give a specific answer to that question, but it does give a clear principle in Ephesians 5:15–17: *"Therefore be careful how you walk, not as unwise men but as wise, making the most of your time, because the days are evil. So then do not be foolish, but understand what the will of the Lord is."*

You have to be wise when it comes to boundaries. Wisdom comes from God. When you set your boundaries, do not set them based on the question "How far is too far?" Set your boundaries based on the question, "What is the wise thing for me to do?" When you know the wise thing, you know where to draw the line. Don't be afraid to voice your boundaries to the guy you are dating. If he is not committed to the same boundaries, it could become extremely difficult to remain pure.

Proverbs 25:28 says, *"A person without self-control is as defenseless as a city with broken-down walls"* (NLT). Be prepared to fight for purity. Do not enter into a dating relationship unarmed.

Have you ever thought about your wedding day? For years, I looked through bridal magazines and tore out pictures of what I wanted to wear on that special day. As part of the church, you are the bride of Christ. Have you ever thought about what you are wearing as the bride of Christ? Psalm 29:2 says, *"Give to the Lord the glory due to His name; worship the Lord in the beauty of holiness or in holy array"* (AMP). We are to adorn ourselves with holiness. Our wedding dresses are to be constructed of holiness. A white wedding gown symbolizes purity. We are to worship the Lord dressed in holiness and purity.

I encourage you to picture yourself as a bride who is preparing herself for her wedding. One day, a trumpet will sound, and it will be your heavenly wedding day. On that day everything—all the details—will have been handled. All the trials, heartaches, and pains of getting ready for the big event will pay off. The Church will finally see her bridegroom, Jesus Christ, face to face. On that day, I pray you will be glowing because you have chosen not to cover up or compensate for poor vision with impurity of heart. Instead you have chosen to walk the path of purity.

Perfectionism

Not only do girls cover up with immodesty and impurity, but we often disguise the condition of our hearts with perfectionism. The perfectionist will stop at nothing to achieve that personal goal of perfection. Seeking excellence is not bad in itself, but more times than not, we have the wrong standard of excellence in our minds. Do you believe you will be loved only if you are perfect? First John 4:19 says, *"We love, because He first loved us."* God loves us already, and we can do nothing more to make Him love us. God doesn't care what size you are or about other physical characteristics. He just loves you as you are. You do not have to be perfect to have His love and attention.

I once counseled a girl who was in the midst of battling anorexia. She is a beautiful, talented, intelligent girl who has had the most blurred vision with regard to herself. She cannot see what she really looks like, and she holds herself to a self-conceived standard of perfection. She lost weight until she became a size 0 in most clothes. I can't even imagine being that size! Recently the clothing store Abercrombie & Fitch released a new size for their stores: it is a size 00! Like one 0 wasn't enough! So this young woman saw 00 as the standard of perfection.

To whose standard are you comparing yourself? Are you comparing yourself to the world's standard of perfection? …Abercrombie & Fitch's standard? Whose? What about God's standard? Are you seeking God's perfection for your life? God's standard and the world's are completely different. We fuel our obsessive mentality when we hold ourselves up to the wrong standard. I do not need to be a size 00 to be loved. God has unfailing love that He freely lavishes on us. He makes all real love possible, and wants us to know love not on the basis of who we are, but on the fact of who He is.

How Do We See God?

A lot of times we operate under a false understanding of who God is. We have a poor picture of Him. We see no difference between man and God. Some people see God as their copilot. Others see Him as a team player. Many times, people envision God as the way they want Him to be.

Isaiah 6:3 described God as holy: *"And one called out to another and said, 'Holy, Holy, Holy, is the LORD of hosts, the whole earth is full of His glory.'"* He is holy. He is unique in His nature. He is omnipotent, omnipresent, omniscient, infinite, and eternal. He is unique in character: fully and unconditionally loving, just, patient, and gracious. God is holy. He is unique in function: He is the only one who could and did create everything that exists. He is the only one who was able to rescue creation from the effect of sin. God is the only one who possesses all these characteristics. God is to be revered as set apart from other things. That's what it means to be holy—to be set apart from sin. Holiness is the central characteristic of God in the Old Testament.

Not only is God holy, He is also beautiful. The Old Testament describes God as the epitome of beauty. Psalm 27:4 says, *"One thing I have asked from the LORD, that I shall seek: That I may dwell in the house of the LORD all the days of my life, to behold the beauty of the LORD and to meditate in His temple."* The psalmist wanted to behold His beauty. We can behold His beauty every day.

I love to go for walks. I experience God every time I walk because I always behold some aspect of His beauty. Go outside and look around you. What do you see? Can you see His majesty in the clouds? Do you feel Him in the wind? Can you hear the crickets praising Him?

> *The Lord is good to all, and His tender mercies are over all His works [the entirety of things created]. All Your works shall praise You, O Lord, and Your loving ones shall bless You [affectionately and gratefully shall Your saints confess and praise You]!*
> —Psalm 145:9–10 (AMP)

Doesn't this Scripture make you just want to praise the Lord? Then do!

When I think about how great God is, it makes me realize how small I am. I had the opportunity to go to a tiny island in the South Pacific to speak at a youth rally. This place was the essence of paradise. While I was there, I became sick. I couldn't go one minute without coughing. I was a wreck. I remember being bummed about the fact that I was sick and so far from home. I know that some of you don't feel too sad for me because after all, I was on an island paradise. Let me tell you, it is possible to be bummed in paradise. As I was pouting and complaining to the Lord, I looked up and finally saw the natural beauty that was all around me. In that moment, I caught a glimpse of something I needed to be reminded of—**God's bigness**. I realized how small I was and how insignificant my worries were. How many times in the course of a week do you realize God's bigness? To understand how to respect God with your body, you must first come to an understanding of who He is and who you are not.

Sacrifice Your Cover-Ups

We need to sacrifice to God everything we use as a cover-up or disguise. Let me explain. Deep within us, we all want to nurse our hurts. We don't feel good about our body, we don't feel beautiful, and so we use things like immodesty, impurity, or perfectionism as disguises to make us feel better. When it comes to taking care of our heart, God asks us to make a sacrifice, and that sacrifice is to overcome the desire to make ourselves feel better by hiding behind these false cover-ups or a whole host of other disguises. We need to let go and let God mend our heart.

A friend told me once that I wasn't making a sacrifice unless I was giving up something I liked or wanted. I already told you I liked guys making me feel beautiful. I liked getting a response from guys by the way I dressed. I liked the way I felt when things "seemed" to be perfect. But it wasn't until I learned to sacrifice my disguises that God began to do a work in my heart. He began to satisfy my desire to be known as beautiful.

Perceive God's Truth

Some of us have covered up the issues of our heart by believing lies about beauty and our appearance for so long, we've lost our ability to perceive truth. I believe there is a direct correlation between our eyes and our mind. What we see—either physically or spiritually—determines our perspectives on things. If I don't wear my contacts, my perception of the road on which I drive looks completely different than if I'm wearing my lenses. If we don't wear God's glasses or corrective lenses (see things from His perspective), then we will perceive our body differently than what is actually true.

What if I could hear only what God thinks of me rather than what I perceive to be what the world thinks of me? What difference would it make in my perception of my body? I believe it would make a huge difference if I could hear only God's truth, not the world's lies. When I get a mani-cure, I go to a place run by wonderful Korean people. While I'm sitting there, they talk to each other in their native language. I don't speak Korean, and so I can't understand what they are saying. That's how I want to be with lies. I want lying and believing lies to be so foreign to me that I can't understand a single word. I pray the same for you.

> *Some of us have lost our ability to perceive truth.*

When I look at the world around me and compare myself with other women, whether they are my roommates or celebrities, I begin to hate my appearance. I am tempted to adapt myself to the world's standard. This response is not strange to women. Women everywhere adapt themselves in such ways as cosmetic surgery, expensive clothes, excessive jewelry, or body piercing. Our culture has given us an *unreachable* standard to attain. It is also an *unreasonable* standard because it is ever shifting. The standard of today will probably not be the standard five years into the future. As Christians, we are not to live according to the world's standard. First Samuel 16:7 says, *"God sees not as man sees, for man looks at the outward appearance, but the LORD looks at the heart."* Our beauty is not determined by man. Our beauty and worth are established by God Almighty, the Creator of heaven and earth.

Bible Study Questions

1   Memorize Psalm 45:11. Write it down on a card, and carry it with you this week in order to remind yourself of God's truth.

2   Why do you think every woman longs to be beautiful?

3   What does the Bible say about beauty in Proverbs 31:30 and Psalm 45:11?

4   What causes you to have blurred vision? What are the effects of your blurred vision?

5   Which disguise do you use to cover up: immodesty, impurity, perfectionism, or other?

6   Read 1 Peter 3:3–5. What is precious in the eyes of God? What is a gentle spirit?

7   Read 1 Samuel 16:7. What does your heart look like? Have you put more focus on your outward appearance than on your heart?

8   Read Psalm 145:1–13. What is your view of God? Describe Him.

9   Read Leviticus 11:44–45 and 1 Samuel 2:2. God is holy and deserves our respect. Do you respect God with your body?

Body. Beauty. Boys.

Write your reactions to Sarah's thoughts in this chapter. Which thoughts relate to you? Which ones don't relate to you? How did you feel as you read?

_____

_____

_____

_____

_____

_____

_____

_____

_____

_____

_____

_____

_____

_____

_____

_____

_____

55

CHAPTER THREE

Lies I Believed and the Truth That Set Me Free

Do you ever wish you had someone else's identity? Even as a little girl, I can remember taking on the identity of other persons. I would have liked to have been Kelly Ripa. She has the life I've always wanted. My dream job would be to host a morning talk show with Regis. In fact, I'm a little like Kelly. I say those dumb blonde things that make people laugh. I think Regis would have fun laughing with me. Kelly has a wardrobe to die for. I love all her clothes. I am a fashion fanatic, so I watch the first few minutes of their show every morning just to see what Kelly is wearing. But in reality, none of us can assume another's identity.

Identity Issues

Has someone ever tried to take your identity? As a child, I had a neighbor who tried to be me. It drove me crazy. She wanted everything I had. She said everything I said. One year, I got a new baby doll for Christmas. He was a newborn, and I named him Steve. I was a proud mother. My neighbor girl saw him and convinced her father to buy her one. Guess what she named him? Steve! She was searching for identity and tried to find it in me.

For many years, I didn't really know who I was. Oh, I knew my name and where I lived and that kind of stuff. I also knew that I had trusted Christ as my Savior and that I was going to heaven. But I never really saw myself the way God saw me. I lived under a false identity. I believed the lies that Satan told me.

Understanding our identity is absolutely essential to successfully living the Christian life. Knowing who we are in Christ is one of the most liberating truths we will ever understand. Let me ask you this: What do these three people have in common?

1. Shaquille O'Neal the athlete
2. Britney Spears the singer
3. Jennifer Aniston the actress

I know you can think of many commonalities. They're all celebrities. They're all wealthy. They're all attractive. But the answer I want to reveal to you is that their identity is based on their performance. Shaq plays basketball. Britney sings and dances. Jennifer acts. We tend to judge people according to their performance. Since we judge each other that way, it's easy for us to assume that God would judge us according to our performance or behavior. But God doesn't judge us the same way—He doesn't judge us according to our performance. He determines our identity by our birth. (I'm not talking about physical birth here.) He determines our identity by our spiritual birth. John 3:3 says, *"In reply Jesus declared, 'I tell you the truth, no one can see the kingdom of God unless he is born again'"* (NIV). Jesus meant that after your physical birth, there must come a time when you are born again, born of the Spirit—a time when you receive *new* life. The time must come when the old you goes and the new you comes.

> Knowing who we are in Christ is one of the most liberating truths we will ever understand.

Second Corinthians 5:17 says, *"Therefore, if anyone is in Christ, he is a new creation; the old has gone, the new has come!"* (NIV). The root word for creation is "create." The word doesn't mean to improve something that already exists. It means to bring something into being out of nothing. God didn't simply change you when you became a Christian. He created a brand new you. Your outward appearance didn't change, your personality didn't change, but He gave you a new identity.

Lies Versus the Truth: Sources of Each

I battled a poor body image for many years because I never understood my identity in Christ. I believed many lies Satan told me. Our culture is riddled with deception. Everywhere we turn we are bombarded with half-truths, misconceptions, and flat-out lies. Sometimes I can't sleep at night, so I end up watching infomercials: for example, "Look better and feel younger in just 10 minutes a day…the key to a healthier, happier life." That was an ad for an oxygen chamber! Who needs it? Magazine covers trick us: "A better you in one week!" "Melt 10 lbs in 10 minutes." Lies are all around us.

Sometimes it's easy to see through the falsehood of advertisements. Unfortunately, most lies are not that easy to detect. Deceptive ads appeal to our human wants and longings. We *want* to believe that somehow, someway, mysteriously, those unwanted pounds really could melt away in just 10 minutes—no sweat, no pain, no effort. Am I right? That's why we watch the advertisements and infomercials.

Satan was the very first advertising agent. In a clever way, he changed Adam's and Eve's thinking about God. You could call his scheme the first false-advertising campaign. Satan wanted to drive a wedge between God and His people. He knew that in order to do that, he would have to deceive them. Let's check out the following report on how it happened with Eve and how it could happen to us:

> *I hope you will put up with a little of my foolishness; but you are already doing that. I am jealous for you with a godly jealousy. I promised you to one husband, to Christ, so that I might present you as a pure virgin to him. But I am afraid that just as Eve was deceived [seduced] by the serpent's cunning, your minds may somehow be led astray from your sincere and pure devotion to Christ.*
> —1 Corinthians 11:1–3 (NIV)

Satan's plan is to seduce and entice us away from the truth as he did Eve. Being clever, he first raised a question in Eve's mind about what God had said. Genesis 3:1 says, *"Now the serpent was more crafty than any beast of the field which the LORD God had made. And he said to the woman, 'Indeed, has God said, "You shall not eat from any tree of the garden"?'"* This is where he began to trick Eve. The fact is that God had told Adam (so Eve's info was hearsay anyway), that he was free to eat of any tree of the garden except one specific tree (Genesis 2:16–17). Once Satan caused Eve to question, he then offered her a lovely plate of "mixed fruit"—a little truth mixed with enticing lies. *"The serpent said to the woman, 'You surely will not die! For God knows that in the day you eat from it your eyes will be opened, and you will be like God, knowing good and evil'"* (Genesis 3:4–5). Satan wants you to believe lies painted up like freedom, so that you will *not* be free, but God wants you to experience true freedom brought about by grace. That's why He sent Jesus.

> *The Word became flesh and made his dwelling among us. We have seen his glory, the glory of the One and Only, who came from the Father, full of grace and truth. John testifies concerning him. He cries out, saying, "This was he of whom I said, 'He who comes after me has surpassed me because he was before me.'" From the fullness of his grace we have all received one blessing after another. For the law was given through Moses; grace and truth came through Jesus Christ. No one has ever seen God, but God the One and Only, who is at the Father's side, has made him known.*
> —John 1:14–18 (NIV)

Twice this passage says that Jesus was full of grace and truth. He came so that you could experience grace and truth and life more abundantly (John 10:10). An abundant life is embodied by freedom. And freedom is "the absence of necessity; not bound; without obstacles; to act without compulsion." Slavery is bondage. Some young women live in a state of bondage because they believe lies. They are deceived. They have been led astray. I don't want you to be deceived.

When I was in high school and college, I sought acceptance through the approval of guys. I wanted so badly to be wanted. I believed the lie that if I made out with guys and gave myself physically, then it would prove that I was pretty. I exchanged the truth of God for a lie. I was deceived just like Eve was deceived. I was led astray from the right way. There is a progression—a gradual change from one state to another—that happens when you are deceived.

Deception is the practice of deliberately making somebody believe things that are not true. Deception can be an act, a trick, or a device. The path to deception begins when you open yourself up to lies. You listen to what Satan says about you. "You're not pretty." "You're not smart." "No one loves you." Then, you obsess about the lies. You dwell on them. You let your mind meditate on the lies Satan fed you. Then you put your faith in the lies. You believe that what Satan said about you is true. You begin to believe you aren't pretty or loved. Worst of all, you begin to act on those lies.

Yes, faith leads to action—that's true in good things or bad things. Having faith in God leads to acting like a child of God. Having faith in a lie that says you aren't pretty leads to acting like you have no confidence. Do you see the progression? It begins with simply opening your ears to what is false. The world tries to deceive us, but God offers us something real. This real truth comes through grace. The promises of God flow from His graciousness.

Grace and truth come though Jesus Christ: *"For the law was given through Moses; grace and truth came through Jesus Christ"* (John 1:17 NIV).

To fully understand where truth comes from, we need to understand where lies come from: Satan, the devil, our adversary. Jesus describes Satan (the devil) as *"a liar and the father of lies"* (John 8:44). We will look at that passage closer after we check out the vivid mental picture Peter painted of Satan:

> *Be of sober spirit, be on the alert. Your adversary, the devil, prowls around like a roaring lion, seeking someone to devour. But resist him, firm in your faith, knowing that the same experiences of suffering are being accomplished by your brethren who are in the world.*
> —1 Peter 5:8–9

Look at how Satan is described by Peter. He is not a cute little kitten. He is a roaring lion who lies in wait to kill you…to devour you. Peter's advice is to resist him, to be firm in your faith. To be firm against his onset means to be rooted, established, strong, immovable, and determined.

Now let's look again at the way Jesus described the devil:

> *You are of your father the devil, and you want to do the desires of your father. He was a murderer from the beginning, and does not stand in the truth because there is no truth in him. Whenever he speaks a lie, he speaks from his own nature, for he is a liar and the father of lies. But because I speak the truth, you do not believe Me.*
> —John 8:44–45

Jesus describes Satan, calling him the devil, *"a liar and the father of lies."* It's easy to become rooted in lies. I was for more than a decade.

My father owns a plant nursery. I've been around plants and trees all my life. One thing I know about trees is that they have roots. When a tree has been rooted for a long time, it is difficult to uproot. If you were to uproot a tree, the first thing you would want to do is to note the type of soil in which a tree is rooted. If a tree is in a dry soil, it is difficult for it to grow because there is no water. We need to be a tree rooted in the right soil. When we are deceived, it's like being rooted in lies instead of being rooted in truth. Our roots have no water. The longer that we are rooted in lies, the harder it is to pull up the root.

> *Think about where you are rooted.*

> *For he will be like a bush in the desert*
> *And will not see when prosperity comes,*
> *But will live in stony wastes in the wilderness,*
> *A land of salt without inhabitant.*
> *Blessed is the man who trusts in the* LORD
> *And whose trust is the* LORD.
> *For he will be like a tree planted by the water,*
> *That extends its roots by a stream*
> *And will not fear when the heat comes;*
> *But its leaves will be green,*
> *And it will not be anxious in a year of drought*
> *Nor cease to yield fruit.*
> —Jeremiah 17:6–8

God wants us to be rooted in truth so that when the heat of deception comes we will not wither. Think about where you are rooted. Are you rooted in lies or truth?

Three Principles of Covenant

When we accept Christ as our Savior, we enter into covenant with Him. Because of this covenant, lies are dispelled and truth is highlighted. Christ made a new covenant with us. It's a covenant of grace. Covenant teaches us identity and oneness.

Now it came about when he had finished speaking to Saul, that the soul of Jonathan was knit to the soul of David, and Jonathan loved him as himself. Saul took him that day and did not let him return to his father's house. Then Jonathan made a covenant with David because he loved him as himself. Jonathan stripped himself of the robe that was on him and gave it to David, with his armor, including his sword and his bow and his belt. So David went out wherever Saul sent him, and prospered; and Saul set him over the men of war. And it was pleasing in the sight of all the people and also in the sight of Saul's servants.
—1 Samuel 18:1–5

In this passage, we see Jonathan and David make a covenant. In the Old Testament, when two entered into a covenant, they exchanged robes to symbolize their covenant. For example: If we were sitting together and both wearing jackets, to establish our covenant, I would ask you to exchange jackets with me. This is what Jonathan and David did. I want to show you three principles that exchanging robes or jackets symbolizes.

Principle 1: Change of Identity

The first principle that exchanging robes symbolizes is a **total change of identity.** In the preceding passage, verse one said that the soul of Jonathan was knit to the soul of David. When I think of something being knit together, I think of a scarf. Yarn is intertwined and woven together. I think it's interesting that the author described their souls as being woven together. When Jonathan exchanged robes with David, their souls were united. They became as one.

What does a total change of identity look like? Let's go back to you and me swapping jackets. When two people exchange jackets, something interesting happens. Whatever you owe, I owe, and vice versa. All that you own, I now own and vice versa. Think about that for a minute. You're getting a good deal. You now own a Honda Accord—my Honda Accord. I've taken great care of it so it won't be a problem for you. You have an outstanding wardrobe from which to choose. On the flip side of things, your rent is due in a couple of days along with all the other monthly bills. Remember, all that I owe, you owe, and all that I own, you own. It's pretty amazing how that works! Now, here's the cool part—think about that truth with Jesus. The Bible says that we have entered into covenant with Jesus. A covenant is a contract or a binding agreement. Everything I owe, He owed and paid, and everything He has became mine. That's a much more amazing deal for both you and me.

Principle 2: Total Commitment

The second principle that I want you to see is that exchanging robes symbolizes a **total commitment to each other**. Once again, think back to the phrase "knit together." You have been knit or bound together with Christ.

Not long ago, I was at a Christmas party. Everyone was supposed to bring a white elephant gift. One girl opened up a pair of handcuffs. It was hilarious. At the end of the night, she decided to link herself with me. It was funny for a while until I needed to use the restroom. That's where I drew the line. The handcuffs had to come off! Being linked with handcuffs is not fun after awhile. But being linked with Jesus is a whole different story. That link eliminates fear. That link gives us eternal security with Christ. You cannot be separated from His love, mercy, forgiveness, or grace. When you enter into a covenant relationship with Christ, you become knitted, bound together with Him. You are in total commitment to Him and He is to you.

Principle 3: Unselfish Love

The third principle I want you to see is that exchanging robes symbolizes **total, unselfish love.** A covenant takes two persons. The persons involved in this story are Jonathan and David. Jonathan initiated the covenant with David. The truth is that the story says much more about the one who initiated than the one who received. Jonathan was heir to the throne. He was King Saul's son. David was just a shepherd. Jonathan had a lot to lose, and David had a lot to gain.

For us, exchanging robes with God says a lot about His unselfish love for us. What has God done to initiate a covenant with man? He sent His one and only Son to die for mankind. John 3:16 says, *"For God so loved the world, that He gave His only begotten Son, that whoever believes in Him shall not perish, but have eternal life."* In much the same way that Jonathan initiated covenant with David, God initiated covenant with us.

I picture our covenant with God like a marriage covenant. A time of dating leads up to the wedding day. I once dated a guy named Shaun. I was blown away at how he pursued me. I had never had someone do that before. I knew that I wanted to be pursued, but all the other guys around seemed to be hot glued to their seats. Then Shaun came after me with all he had, and I liked it. It was so romantic. That's how God is with us. He pursues us. He is continually pursuing us. He wants a covenant relationship with us. He initiates it, and it's the most romantic thing we can ever experience.

Not long ago, I had a couple of rough weeks. One day, I was sitting in my office on the verge of tears for no apparent reason. A lady who works at the church walked into my office with a dozen roses of all different colors. They were beautiful. She brought them to me because she thought they would be pretty in my office. Then, I really had a reason to cry! I knew that they were really from the One who pursues me and the covenant relationship to which we are committed. Every morning, the Lord will satisfy us with His unfailing, unselfish love. He gave us everything. He is totally committed to us.

> Have this attitude in yourselves which was also in Christ Jesus, who, although He existed in the form of God, did not regard equality with God a thing to be grasped, but emptied Himself, taking the form of a bond-servant, and being made in the likeness of men. Being found in appearance as a man, He humbled Himself by becoming obedient to the point of death, even death on a cross. For this reason also, God highly exalted Him, and bestowed on Him the name which is above every name.
> —Philippians 2:5–9

Christ put on our robe of humanity, our robe of sin. He put on our likeness. The reality is that in covenant, two become one. Think of a marriage. Just as a husband and wife become one when they enter into covenant, you and Christ become one when you come into covenant with Him. In entering this covenant, you become a new creation. You have a new identity.

Transformation

The world says that acceptance and completion are all about externals. We women constantly look for acceptance and completion. The world says that we need an external transformation. The world says that to be complete:

- Something has to be done to you.
- Someone has to be with you.
- Circumstances have to be right around you.
- You have to be improved.
- Something has to be said about you.
- You have to own more things, have more titles.
- You must achieve more accomplishments.

According to Scripture, it's not about externals, but about an internal transformation. Colossians 3:1–3 says, *"Therefore if you have been raised up with Christ, keep seeking the things above, where Christ is, seated at the right hand of God. Set your mind on the things above, not on the things that are on earth. For you have died and your life is hidden with Christ in God."* Your life is in Christ. I didn't change on the outside when I became a Christian. An internal transformation happened. It's not as if I once was an extrovert, and now that I'm a Christian I'm an introvert. The external stayed the same, but my heart changed.

We learn about this internal transformation in the Bible. Scripture tells us that we need to put on the new identity He gave us. You're probably thinking, *that's great, but how do I put on spiritual clothes (identity) and what do they look like?* Over and over, we see the words *"put on"* in Scripture.

> *That, in reference to your former manner of life, you lay aside the old self, which is being corrupted in accordance with the lusts of deceit, and that you be renewed in the spirit of your mind, and put on the new self, which in the likeness of God has been created in righteousness and holiness of the truth.*
> —Ephesians 4:22–24

To *put on* means to get dressed, to be clothed. Think about how you get dressed in the morning. You *put on* clothes. God is saying that we need to do that spiritually. We need to put on the new outfit that He gave us. I want you to read a passage that Paul wrote to Christians at Colossae about what to put aside and what to put on:

*"But now you also, put them all aside: anger, wrath, malice, slander, and abusive speech from your mouth. Do not lie to one another, since you laid aside the old self with its evil practices, and have put on the new self who is being renewed to a true knowledge according to the image of the One who created him—renewal in which there is no distinction between Greek and Jew, circumcised and uncircumcised, barbarian, Scythian, slave and freeman, but Christ is all, and in all. So, as those who have been **chosen** of God, **holy** and **beloved**, put on a heart of compassion, kindness, humility, gentleness and patience; bearing with one another, and forgiving each other, whoever has a complaint against anyone; just as the Lord forgave you, so also should you. Beyond all these things put on love, which is the perfect bond of unity."*
—Colossians 3:8–14 (bold added for emphasis)

From this passage, I want to show you three words that describe your new identity: *chosen, holy, and beloved.*

New Identity

The first word for your new identity is **chosen.** God picked you. You are accepted, approved, and significant. You no longer have to walk into a room and look for acceptance. God accepts you…now…as you are. When I grasped this truth, it cut to the marrow of my bones.

One Sunday in early spring when I was 21 years old, I was home in Tennessee visiting my family. I was sitting in the worship service at my home church. As the pastor was speaking, I was daydreaming (embarrassing, but true). I began to look at my left hand and gaze at my ring finger. There was no ring on that finger. I began to think, *One day, you'll have something sparkly on that hand. One day, someone will pick you.* As I was thinking that to myself, the Lord began to speak to my heart. He said: *Sarah, what are you talking about? I have already picked you! I have chosen you. You don't need to wait for some man to pick you. It's already happened.* I went out the next day and bought a ring from James Avery. It's a simple silver ring with a cross embossed in it. I put it on my ring finger on my left hand to symbolize being chosen of God. Every morning thereafter, when I put on that ring, I remembered that God had picked me. Even if no earthly man picked me, God had chosen me.

Some of you have spent your life wanting to be picked, approved, accepted, chosen. But is has already happened. Remember what God has done for you. Remember, He exchanged robes with you. Renew your mind and believe what you know to be true. Put off the old self and keep putting on the new.

The second new identity word is **holy.** To be holy means to be pure. You are clean. Your sins are washed away. Colossians 1:13–14 says, *"For He rescued us from the domain of darkness, and transferred us to the kingdom of His beloved Son, in whom we have redemption, the forgiveness of sins."* When you became a Christian, Christ rescued you from destruction and transferred you to a new life, a clean life, a holy life.

Something interesting happens when you are transferred. Transfers happen all the time in sports. Players are transferred to other teams. What happens when a player is transferred? He moves to a new city to play for a new team. He wears a new uniform and learns new plays. He has a new identity. He is no longer part of the former team. That's what happened to you when you became a Christian. You joined a new team. What identity or "uniform" is in your closet? Do you wear the clothes that resemble failure, rejection, loss, or guilt? Remember, you were made in the image of God. You have a new identity. You are someone who can still sin, but you're not a sinner anymore. Now you are holy because of what Christ did on the cross.

The third identity word that describes you is **beloved**. You are loved by God. The literal translation of *beloved* means "to be content with." God is content with you. He is satisfied with you. You are not rejected. *"May the beloved of the LORD dwell in security by Him, who shields him all the day, and he dwells between His shoulders"* (Deuteronomy 33:12).

Almost every girl thinks about finding the man of her dreams. We dream of being romanced. After a period of dating, we hope to get engaged with a beautiful 1.5 carat round-cut diamond ring. (What? You say you prefer oval, pear, or square? To each her own.) Then we have the wedding of our dreams, and a life of togetherness follows. After being married for a few years, you hope for two kids. You hope to enjoy life and grow old together. I assume this is the dream most of you have. We all want someone to be intimate with us and to never leave us. We

Body, Beauty, Boys

all crave unfailing love. In Christ, you have unfailing love. You are His beloved.

Most girls love to get new clothes. I want to wear a new outfit as soon as I get it home from the store. Imagine for a moment with me that you married a wonderful man, and he bought you new clothes. Wouldn't it be silly to continue wearing the same old outfit over and over and leave the new clothes hanging in the closet? Imagine what your husband would think? Don't you think he would be saddened by your lack of interest in the new clothes he bought you? He just spent a bundle to buy you that new wardrobe. Maybe you like the shoes he bought, but you still wear the old shirt from the discount store even though he bought you a Dolce & Gabbana shirt. It's in the closet just waiting for you to put it on. That's how we sometimes are in our relationship with God. We may believe that we are loved by God, but not believe that we are holy or accepted. We must learn to put on the clothes He gives…put on the whole outfit. Our job is simply to get dressed.

You are chosen, holy, and beloved.

When I first began to wear my new identity, I put the three words that describe that new identity—chosen, holy, and beloved—everywhere so that I would see them; I put them on my mirror, in my closet, on the refrigerator, on my desk, on the dashboard of my car. Whenever I saw them, I would read them and renew my mind to the truth. We must put on that truth that we are *chosen, holy,* and *beloved.*

Get dressed every day…in the right clothes. Understanding your identity frees you to accept who you are and to become the person God created you to be. Knowing your real identity is absolutely essential to your success in having a good body image.

Bible Study Questions

1   Memorize Colossians 3:12. Write the words *chosen, holy,* and *beloved* on note cards, and place them where you will see them often.

2   If you could change identity with anyone, who would it be and why?

3   Where do you think your identity is based? What kind of things define you?

4   What do you think the world says about your identity?

5   Read 2 Corinthians 5:17. What strikes you about this verse?

6   Read Colossians 3:12; 1 Corinthians 1:2; Ephesians 2:10; Romans 5:17; and Ephesians 1:6. What does the Bible say about your identity?

7   What can you do to help you live according to your identity in Christ?

Body. Beauty. Boys.

Write your reactions to Sarah's thoughts in this chapter. Which thoughts relate to you? Which ones don't relate to you? How did you feel as you read?

_____

_____

_____

_____

_____

_____

_____

_____

_____

_____

_____

_____

_____

_____

_____

_____

_____

A Portrait of Freedom

The mind is the control center for the entire body. Have you ever put your hand on a hot stove? Your mind told you to jerk your hand away. Let me share with you one time that my mind brought about a corresponding action.

After I graduated from college, I worked for a minor league baseball team. The games would usually end around 10:00 P.M. My co-worker and I would then calculate the money from the gift shop. I usually left the ballpark around midnight.

After a game one night, I was driving home and got stuck in traffic. So much traffic that late at night was highly unusual. The last thing I wanted to do was to sit in a traffic jam, as I had to be back at the ballpark early the next morning. I decided to take an alternate route—one that I had sometimes taken in the morning on my way to work, but I had never taken it after dark. This alternate route took me straight through a dangerous neighborhood of Chattanooga, Tennessee. As I drove through this neighborhood, so many people were just hanging out, lining the streets and sitting on cars, that I couldn't get through quickly. I crept down the street. Uncomfortable thoughts came to my mind: There I was—a young woman…all alone…in a little red sports car…looking clueless. I must look like a perfect candidate for an attack! The thoughts entering my mind caused me to fear. My mind began sending out alert signals: Danger! Beware! Then my fear led me to get out of that area as quickly as possible.

Your mind is also the control center for your emotions. Your mind tells you when you are happy, sad, or angry. And emotions lead to actions.

God wants us to glorify Him through our actions, so that means we must first seek to glorify Him with our mind and with our emotions.

Loving God with Heart, Soul, and Mind

When we glorify God with our mind and emotions, we experience freedom in the area of body image.

> *"Teacher, which is the great commandment in the Law?" And He said to him, "'You shall love the LORD your God with all your heart, and with all your soul, and with all your mind.' This is the great and foremost commandment. The second is like it, 'You shall love your neighbor as yourself.'"*
> —Matthew 22:36–39

These verses say to love God with all your heart, soul, and mind. That means that everything we do should be for His sake, to glorify Him. How do we glorify God with our mind? We glorify God with our mind by choosing what we think about. Remember, our thoughts will lead to actions. What do you think about your body? What do you think about your personality? If you hate your body, to what action will that emotion lead?

King David talked to his son, Solomon, about this principle as he passed the torch of leadership to him. Here is David's advice to Solomon shortly before his son became king:

> *"So now I charge you in the sight of all Israel and of the assembly of the LORD, and in the hearing of our God: Be careful to follow all the commands of the LORD your God, that you may possess this good land and pass it on as an inheritance to your descendants forever. And you, my son Solomon, acknowledge the God of your father, and serve him with wholehearted devotion and with a willing mind, for the LORD searches every heart and understands every motive behind the thoughts. If you seek him, he will be found by you; but if you forsake him, he will reject you forever. Consider now, for the LORD has chosen you to build a temple as a sanctuary. Be strong and do the work."*
> —1 Chronicles 28:8–10 (NIV)

In this passage, to have a willing mind means "to delight in; be pleased with; desire." God desires that you delight in Him. What does it mean to delight in something? Think about the things that bring you delight— that make you smile. Think about the things that are absolutely the most fun to you; they are delights to you.

One way I delight in God is by enjoying His creation. A sunset is one of my all-time favorite things to see. Sunsets are so incredibly beautiful. When you give God your whole heart—when you find your delight in Him, you will be amazed at the sweet things He will do to show favor to you.

We were created in the image of God and that means we are to be like Him. We are to represent Him in all we do. God wants us to represent His mind. 1 Corinthians 2:16 says, *"For who has known the mind of the LORD, that he will instruct Him? But we have the mind of Christ."* God's Word says that we are to have the mind of Christ—not just a good mind, not just a mind that scores the highest on tests, but the very mind of Christ!

If you are a Christian, that verse should describe you. You should have the mind of Christ. Christ lives inside you, and because He does, you get everything that He is. You have the ability to think like Christ and therefore act like Christ. Philippians 2:5 says, *"Have this attitude in yourselves which was also in Christ Jesus."* The word for *attitude* in this verse means *mind*. We are not to just resemble Him—we are to think like Him.

Do you have a little sister or brother? Most younger siblings want to be and act just like older siblings. They mimic everything the older siblings do. They copy everything said by the older sibling. In fact, the copying can become quite annoying. As a child I often got into trouble because I would tag along with my older brother. I would wear his clothes. I would talk like him. I would do whatever he did. That's a good picture of how we are to be with Christ. We are to follow Him around, talk like Him, act like Him, and think like Him. The difference between the typical older sibling and Him is that He never gets annoyed with our copying Him.

Jesus embodies a life of freedom. Having the same attitude as Jesus ensures that we will have an attitude of freedom. And what is freedom? Freedom is the absence of necessity. It is not being bound by anything. It is being without obstacles. It is boldness. It is the ability to act without compulsion. Think about these definitions. Does your life exhibit freedom? Are you free to love all of yourself or do you act out of compulsion? Many women who battle poor body image are acting out of compulsion. They eat or don't eat out of compulsion. They exercise out of compulsion. They are slaves to their compulsions. To be a slave is to be in bondage—no freedom there. God promises us freedom.

> *The Spirit of the Sovereign LORD is on me,*
> *because the LORD has anointed me*
> *to preach good news to the poor.*
> *He has sent me to bind up the brokenhearted,*
> *to proclaim freedom for the captives*
> *and release from darkness for the prisoners.*
> —Isaiah 61:1 (NIV)

> *It was for freedom that Christ set us free; therefore keep*
> *standing firm and do not be subject again to a yoke of slavery.*
> —Galatians 5:1

Freedom in the Form of Grace

For years, Satan deceived me about my appearance, but God gave me His truth and through grace I was set free. *"To the Jews who had believed him, Jesus said, 'If you hold to my teaching, you are really my disciples. Then you will know the truth, and the truth will set you free'"* (John 8:31–32 NIV). God's grace is available to set you free, too.

The English transliteration of the Greek word for grace is *charis*. In the Greek, the word means "unmerited favor." The word *grace* appears 125 times in the New Testament. *Unmerited* means "undeserved or unearned." God has given us the gift of freedom. That gift comes in the form of grace.

There is a story in the Bible (John 4:1–26) that paints a portrait of freedom for us. This is the story of the Samaritan woman who met freedom face to face. Jesus was traveling from village to village preaching about the kingdom of God. He wanted all people to experience an extraordinary life. He described the people as being distressed and, referring to the writings of Isaiah the prophet, lost like sheep without a shepherd (Isaiah 53:6).

Jesus came to Samaria, a region north of Jerusalem. The Jews and Samaritans didn't have a good relationship. The Samaritans were a mixed race, part Gentile and part Jew. Jews in Jesus's time looked down on Samaritans with racial and religious contempt. The hatred ran deep, but that didn't stop Jesus. He saw this Samaritan woman at the well and asked her for a drink of water. Then, He offered her living water. She was perplexed that a Jew would, first of all, even talk to her, and then offer living water:

> *Jesus answered and said to her, "Everyone who drinks of this water will thirst again; but whoever drinks of the water that I will give him shall never thirst; but the water that I will give him will become in him a well of water springing up to eternal life."*
> —John 4:13–14

When Jesus offered the woman living water, He offered her freedom. She had a terrible past. She was enslaved by sin. The salvation Jesus offers brings freedom *from* sin and freedom *over* sin. When you become a Christian, you are saved from sin, and you also have power over sin. Being enslaved to our appearance is sin, but Jesus offers you freedom from that slavery.

After the Emancipation Proclamation, some slaves chose to remain in slavery because they were afraid of the unknown. I believe we are like that. Sometimes we are scared to live a life of freedom because we don't know what a life of freedom would really look like. What would it be like to not stress over every meal for fear of taking in too many calories? What would it be like to look in the mirror and see God's creation instead of the distorted view of one suffering from an eating disorder? What would it be like to wake up every day in freedom from all of it? Christ came to offer you a life of freedom. On the canvas of your heart, He wants to paint the most beautiful portrait of a freed you.

> *1 What shall we say then? Are we to continue in sin so that grace may increase?*
> *2 May it never be! **How shall we who died to sin still live in it?***
> *3 Or do you not know that all of us who have been baptized into Christ Jesus have been baptized into His death?*

4 Therefore we have been buried with Him through baptism into death, so that as Christ was raised from the dead through the glory of the Father, so we too might walk in newness of life.

5 For if we have become united with Him in the likeness of His death, certainly we shall also be in the likeness of His resurrection,

6 knowing this, that our old self was crucified with Him, in order that our body of sin might be done away with, so that we would no longer be slaves to sin;

7 for he who has died is freed from sin.

8 Now if we have died with Christ, we believe that we shall also live with Him,

9 knowing that Christ, having been raised from the dead, is never to die again; death no longer is master over Him.

10 For the death that He died, He died to sin once for all; but the life that He lives, He lives to God.

11 Even so consider yourselves to be dead to sin, but alive to God in Christ Jesus.

12 Therefore **do not let sin reign in your mortal body** *so that you obey its lusts,*

13 and do not go on presenting the members of your body to sin as instruments of unrighteousness; but present yourselves to God as those alive from the dead, and your members as instruments of righteousness to God.

14 **For sin shall not be master over you,** *for you are not under law but under grace.*

—Romans 6:1–14 (bold added for emphasis)

I love this section of Scripture. In fact, I love it so much that I memorized it. I believe that in these verses, there is much for us to learn about freedom from eating disorders. These verses talk about the fact that Jesus Christ came and conquered death and sin. In verse 2, Paul asked, *"How shall we who died to sin still live in it?"* When you became a Christian, you died to sin. God created and birthed a new you. Because Christ conquered sin, you don't have to be held in bondage to sin. You are no longer in bondage to sin, but you have been made alive in Christ Jesus.

Body. Beauty. Boys.

Verse 12 in the passage above implores us not to let sin reign in our bodies. That word *reign* means "to have predominance." Predominance means "to have the greatest importance, power, or influence." When we listen to Satan, we allow lies to have the greatest importance and power in our lives. When we are under Satan's influence, the lies he tells us about our appearance dominate what we do and how we live.

> *The power of God that resides within us enables us to live a life of freedom.*

Paul says in verse 14 that we are not to let sin be master over us. When something is your master, you bow down to it. When you believe lies, you bow down not only to those lies, but also to the one who tells them to you. Lies can rule over us, and Paul exhorts us to let only the grace of God rule over us. I want to echo Paul in saying, "*Are we to continue in sin so that grace may increase? May it never be!*" (verses 1–2).

How do we experience freedom? How can we live the Christian life? Colossians 2:6 says, "*So then, just as you received Christ Jesus as Lord, continue to live in him.*" The way you received Christ is the same way you live a life of freedom. How did you receive Him? Philippians 3:10 says, "*That I may know Him and the power of His resurrection and the fellowship of His sufferings, being conformed to His death.*" The word *power* in this verse comes from the Greek word *dunamis*, which is the source for our English word *dynamite*. I believe the power of God that resides within us enables us to live a life of freedom.

Let's investigate the Bible story in Mark 2:1–12 in which Jesus healed a man who was paralyzed. Jesus was teaching a large crowd of people inside a house. While He was teaching, four guys broke open the roof and let down a mat through the ceiling. The funny thing is that someone was lying on that mat! (I cannot imagine what I would think if while I was speaking somewhere, someone all of a sudden was let down through the ceiling!) These four men had brought their friend to Jesus to be healed. The Bible doesn't tell us much about the man on the mat except that he was paralyzed. We don't know how long he had been in this condition. We aren't told whether it happened at birth or later in his life. We aren't even told if *he* wanted to come see Jesus or if his buddies pushed him into doing it. Whatever drove them to action, it was the faith demonstrated by the friends that got Jesus's attention.

"Which is easier, to say to the paralytic, 'Your sins are forgiven'; or to say, 'Get up, and pick up your pallet and walk'? But so that you may know that the Son of Man has authority on earth to forgive sins"—He said to the paralytic, *"I say to you, get up, pick up your pallet and go home." And he got up and immediately picked up the pallet and went out in the sight of everyone, so that they were all amazed and were glorifying God, saying, "We have never seen anything like this."*
—Mark 2:9–12

Jesus just told the guy to get up and walk. What do you think went through the man's head? Did he remember how to walk? Had he ever learned how to walk? However, I don't think he deliberated much about walking because verse 12 says that *"he got up and immediately picked up the pallet and went out in the sight of everyone."* When it comes to being bound by the stronghold of body image obsessiveness, Christ looks at you and says, "Get up and walk—walk in My grace, in My freedom."

Learning to Walk in Grace

How do you get up and walk when you have been in bondage for so long? Do you even know how to walk? Learning to walk in freedom takes grace through faith. Grace is God at work, and faith is active trust.

> *God has given you a credit card of grace with unlimited spending, and yet some of you have never activated God's grace in your life.*

We are actively engaged in depending on Him. Maybe you are afraid to get up and walk because you've lived in defeat for so long. The enemy tries to tell you that you can't even begin to walk in faith. But Jesus says, "Look at Me, and walk this way." The power of grace is activated when you **step out**.

I love blue jeans. I wear them almost every day. Anytime I get some extra money, I spend it on blue jeans. I rarely carry cash, so I most often use my credit card to purchase them. I just received my new credit card in the mail. The card had a sticker on it that instructed me to call a certain number to activate my card. I could have just looked at that new card and admired its beauty and potential, but never activated it. I could have framed it and put it by my bed and just dreamt about the jeans I could someday purchase. Or I could have called the number and activated the card. That's what I did. The credit card would have been useless if I had never activated it. I can't purchase jeans on a card that isn't active.

The same is true with grace. Grace brings freedom, but we need to activate it. God has given you a credit card of grace with unlimited spending, and yet some of you have never activated God's grace in your life. It's as if you framed the credit card of grace, and now you just dream about what it would be like to experience the freedom of using it. Again, grace is activated by our faith.

Acting in Faith

Faith is the confidence that God is who He says He is and that He will do what He says He will do. Faith is the action step of believing. This faith is ongoing. We are continually to believe. He gives power (*dunamis*) to those who believe (Ephesians 1:19).

Faith is believing in something enough to act on it. By faith we totally rely on God, rejecting confidence in ourselves and instead placing our confidence in who God is and in what He says. This is how we are to live in every situation of life. The minute you believe His grace is sufficient for *everything*, the power of grace is released—activated. What will enable you to live a life of freedom? God's grace. You have to believe enough to act on His grace. It's one thing to know God will enable me to stand in front of people and teach, but it is useless if I don't act on it and walk onto the stage. It's easy to say that grace will enable me to experience freedom, but it's useless if I don't take a step.

> In hope against hope he believed, so that he might become a father of many nations according to that which had been spoken, "So shall your descendants be." Without becoming weak in faith he contemplated his own body, now as good as dead since he was about a hundred years old, and the deadness of Sarah's womb; yet, with respect to the promise of God, he did not waver in unbelief but grew strong in faith, giving glory to God, and being fully assured that what God had promised, He was able also to perform.
> —Romans 4:18–21

"In hope against hope," Abraham believed he would be the father of a nation. The odds were against him, yet he did not waver in his faith.

Living in Freedom

How do we begin to live a life of freedom? A few steps I am going to share with you will help you experience a lifestyle of freedom.

Set your mind on things above. The first step to take is to *"Set your mind on the things above, not on the things that are on earth"* (Colossians 3:2).

> *Finally, brethren, whatever is true, whatever is honorable, whatever is right, whatever is pure, whatever is lovely, whatever is of good repute, if there is any excellence and if anything worthy of praise, dwell on these things.*
> —Philippians 4:8

You must set your mind on heavenly values. It's like programming a computer. You predetermine what information the computer will give you by what you program into it. In the same way, you can also program your mind to think on things above. It is not natural to do this. You must make a choice not to grovel in earthly thinking.

We human beings have a will. Our will enables us to obey in spite of our feelings. Most the time, we cannot control our emotions, but we can control our will.

> *We demolish arguments and every pretension that sets itself up against the knowledge of God, and we take captive every thought to make it obedient to Christ.*
> —2 Corinthians 10:5 (NIV)

This verse means that we engage our wills and take control of thoughts that don't glorify God. Whatever enters our mind needs to be put up against God's truth. If it doesn't glorify God, then we need to discard it and *will* our minds to think about those things that do glorify Him.

Cleanse your mind. The second step is to cleanse your mind. The Word of God has a cleansing effect. Just as we need a physical bath every day, we need a spiritual bath every day, too. Jesus said to the disciples, *"You are already clean because of the word which I have spoken to you"* (John 15:3). God cleanses us by His Word. The cleansing effect of the Word is restated in Ephesians 5:25–26: *"Christ loved the church and gave himself up for her to make her holy, cleansing her by the washing with water through the word"* (NIV). Our minds get mixed up with the world's way of thinking, but God's Word cleanses, as it washes away wrong thinking and replaces it with right thinking.

Renew your mind to truth. Along with cleansing our mind, we need to renew our mind to the truth. We've got to actively believe truth. We can't go by how we feel, because emotions are deceptive. Instead we must live by what we know to be true. We have to continually tell our minds the truth to believe.

I love everything about the sky, and I love the sun. I am happiest when it is sunny outside. On occasion when it is gloomy, I become sad. I mope around all day. I can hardly smile. I am not pleasant to be around. This may be a little exaggeration, but I really am sad when the sun does not shine. One day, I love life; the next day, because of some rain, I'm gloomy. But belief doesn't change with the weather. It's like the solid ground under the weather. Belief is something that stays whether we feel good or we feel gloomy. Regardless of the weather, when I step out the door in the morning I believe the ground will be under my feet. God is the ground under my feet, and He's there whether I feel great or not.

> *God is the ground under my feet, and He's there whether I feel great or not.*

Feelings can be deceiving. Our feelings say, "I can't do this…this is too hard…I will never be free…I'm not adequate." This must have been what the paralytic said. I'm sure he didn't *feel* like he could walk, but he *knew* that Jesus had told him to walk. So he trusted the truth rather than his feelings and got up and walked.

> *And do not be conformed to this world, but be transformed by the renewing of your mind, so that you may prove what the will of God is, that which is good and acceptable and perfect.*
> —Romans 12:2

To renew means "to renovate." It means "to make something qualitatively new again." It is a process that brings a complete change for the better. We need to renew our mind, or in other words, we need to renovate our mind. Our mind is the battlefield. That is where we must fight the lies.

Not long ago, my parents began renovating our house. It didn't happen overnight. It was an ongoing process. Every time I came home during that renovating process, something had been changed. I would notice new paint, new wallpaper, and, once, a whole new wall! We have to renovate our minds, too. Piece by piece, we make changes, and soon we have a new mind. We build or construct a mind that believes truth rather than lies.

Possess freedom. God has promised us freedom. It is our promised land. We are to possess freedom. Our country was founded by men who fought for freedom. They passionately pursued it. And that is what we must do. We must pursue and live in the freedom that God has offered us through Christ Jesus. Our promised land is a place of God's unapologetic favor (grace) to us who believe.

In the Old Testament, the promised land was a land flowing with milk and honey. Moses was not allowed to take possession of the land because he failed to believe (Numbers 20:12). Joshua believed, so he was the one chosen to lead the children of Israel into the land. We need to believe that God will do what He has promised. We must believe that He will enable us to be free. We must allow God to renew our minds. His grace is activated by our faith.

Reading the Word of God, which is the living voice of God, is one of the biggest faith builders. Sometimes at night, I can't sleep because my mind is racing with lies. This might sound outrageous, but on those nights I sleep with my Bible. I literally place my head on my Bible as if it were my pillow. I know that God's Word is truth. I want my mind to be thinking and dwelling on truth rather than lies.

> *All things are possible to him who believes.*
> —Mark 9:23

> *To You they cried out and were delivered;*
> *In You they trusted and were not disappointed.*
> —Psalm 22:5

We have to believe the truth about God's grace. *"All things are possible"* when we believe. And when we believe, we will not be *"disappointed."*

Not too long ago, I once again felt disappointed with my appearance, and my disappointment came because I *chose* not to believe God's truth. I felt ugly. I felt fat. I felt disappointed. My life at that time was based on feelings, not truth. God said I will not be disappointed when I believe in Him. So I made the choice to believe God's truth and not to believe my feelings, and things began to come into focus for me. Your feelings will deceive you, but God's truth never will.

Prepare your mind for action. The next step in living a life of freedom is to prepare your mind for action. 1 Peter 1:13 says, *"Therefore, prepare your minds for action; be self-controlled; set your hope fully on the grace to be given you when Jesus Christ is revealed"* (NIV). In some translations, the words *gird up* are used in place of *prepare;* we are to gird up our minds for action. Girding up refers to what had to be done with the long-flowing robes people wore in the first century. People could not run or move quickly in that kind of clothing. Back then, to do anything athletic, a person had to lift the hem of the robe and tuck it under his belt, thus freeing his lower legs for action. This is the picture Peter was trying to illustrate. He's saying that our mind needs to be girded up—to be prepared for action—as if we were going to run a race. Actually, we are running a marathon race called life. Difficult circumstances are going to come our way. Lies are going to bombard us. People will ask us questions about our faith. We need to be prepared for action.

Simply walk. The final step I want to encourage you to follow in living a life of freedom is to simply walk. Just do it! To walk means "to make one's way, to progress." I don't remember learning to walk, but I have watched little ones learn. My niece is 16 months old, and I watched her learn to walk. It's a process. She didn't all of a sudden begin running around the room. She began by crawling, and then her parents stood her up and held her hands as she

> *God doesn't care how many times we fall. He cares about how many times we get back up.*

tried to take a step. They didn't have a flip chart set up to show her how to put one foot in front of the other. Somehow she just knew. She would take a step and fall. She would push herself back up and do the exact same thing again. This pattern happened over and over. Each time she got a little farther. Then one day she was able walk around without falling.

The same is true in our lives. God wants us to learn to walk in truth. We try by putting one foot in front the other, taking baby steps, and sometimes we fall. God doesn't care how many times we fall. He cares about how many times we get back up. The neat thing is that God is the One who gives us the power to walk. Grace is activated when you take a step. May the prayer of your heart be that of the psalmist: *"Teach me Your way, O LORD; I will walk in Your truth"* (Psalm 86:11).

God's grace will enable us to experience a life of freedom. God's grace will enable us to wake up everyday and believe truth. God's grace will enable us to resist the temptation to listen to lies. We just have to recognize where we need grace, believe that God will enable us, and then walk by faith. Every day, activate the freedom found in God's grace. We all have access to it. We just have to walk in it.

Bible Study Questions

1 Memorize Matthew 22:37. Write it down on a card and carry it with you this week.

2 Read Matthew 22:36–39. How can you love God with your all your mind?

3 Read Isaiah 61:1 and Galatians 5:1. What do these verses say about freedom?

4 How do you define faith? How will faith help you find freedom?

5 Read 1 John 2:15–17; 1 Peter 5:8; and Galatians 5:16–17. According to these verses, who are your three enemies?

6 Read 1 John 4:4. How are you encouraged by this verse?

Body. Beauty. Boys.

Write your reactions to Sarah's thoughts in this chapter. Which thoughts relate to you? Which ones don't relate to you? How did you feel as you read?

_____

_____

_____

_____

_____

_____

_____

_____

_____

_____

_____

_____

_____

_____

_____

_____

_____

_____

How to Worship God with Your Body

I want to help you get a new perspective on your body. Maybe sometime in the past you have caught a quick glimpse of God's perspective of you. But most girls have never seen themselves through God's eyes. They see themselves through the eyes of the world. They see themselves as falling short of the standard of beauty.

To be content means "to be satisfied; to be gratified to the full; to be adequate." That's the definition. Now let me ask you this: Do you feel content with you? Do you feel satisfied with who you are? Do you feel adequate? Many times in my life I answered a resounding no to those questions, but now I have found the answer. Now I have the right perspective. I have found a life of contentment in Christ. God promises us contentment. He promises to satisfy us. Let's look at what God's Word says about our source of satisfaction:

> *O satisfy us in the morning with Your lovingkindness,*
> *That we may sing for joy and be glad all our days.*
> —Psalm 90:14

> *How blessed is the one whom You choose and bring near to You*
> *To dwell in Your courts.*
> *We will be satisfied with the goodness of Your house,*
> *Your holy temple.*
> —Psalm 65:4

You open Your hand
And satisfy the desire of every living thing.
—Psalm 145:16

God's Word is full of promises that He will satisfy us.

Sometimes we try to satisfy a spiritual craving in physical ways. Then we wonder why we are never satisfied. We wonder why we are never content. Our life does not have to be like the Rolling Stones song that says, "I can't get no satisfaction." If you are not satisfied with yourself, first of all, know that God made you and loves you as you are and second of all, understand that He wants to satisfy you.

Accepting Yourself

Most of the time when I am discontent with myself, it is because I am holding myself up to the wrong standard. I raise myself up to the world's standard. Every time I compare myself to anyone else—whether celebrity or friend—I am left feeling inadequate and dissatisfied. In chapter one, I talked about my fascination with Hollywood that led me to playing the comparison game. Then, I extended the game to comparing myself with every girl I was around. I reached the point at which I couldn't even see who I was or what I really looked like. I would look in the mirror and not really see what was there. Have you ever experienced a time like that? It was as if I forgot what I looked like when I walked away from the mirror because I constantly held myself up to the wrong standard. One day in my devotional time with the Lord, I read Psalm 139 and realized that God created me to be exactly the way I am. Everything about me was meant to be. I was supposed to look like this. I was supposed to have this personality. I was supposed to have these abilities. I want you to look at these verses with me and allow God to enlighten you with His truth.

1 *O Lord, You have searched me and known me.*
2 *You know when I sit down and when I rise up;*
   You understand my thought from afar.
3 *You scrutinize my path and my lying down,*
   And are intimately acquainted with all my ways.
4 *Even before there is a word on my tongue,*
   Behold, O Lord, You know it all.

5 You have enclosed me behind and before,
   And laid Your hand upon me.
6 Such knowledge is too wonderful for me;
   It is too high, I cannot attain to it.

13 For You formed my inward parts;
   You wove me in my mother's womb.
14 I will give thanks to You, for I am
   fearfully and wonderfully made;
   Wonderful are Your works,
   And my soul knows it very well.
15 My frame was not hidden from You,
   When I was made in secret,
   And skillfully wrought in the depths of the earth;
16 Your eyes have seen my unformed substance;
   And in Your book were all written
   The days that were ordained for me,
   When as yet there was not one of them.
17 How precious also are Your thoughts to me, O God!
   How vast is the sum of them!
18 If I should count them, they would outnumber the sand
   When I awake, I am still with You.

23 Search me, O God, and know my heart;
   Try me and know my anxious thoughts;
24 And see if there be any hurtful way in me,
   And lead me in the everlasting way.
—Psalm 139:1–6, 13–18, 23–24

Did you hear those words about you? I want you to read them again before we move on. I want you to really soak in what God has spoken about you.

Next, I want you to look a little closer at the meaning of some of these words. Verse 3 says that God is *"intimately acquainted"* with all our ways. God knows us inside and out, and He purposely created us just the way we are. Then verse 13 says that God created our *"inward parts."* That literally means our insides—like our kidneys. God knew exactly how our bodies would work or would not work.

When I lived in California, I became very close to a family there. This family had a daughter who was 15 at the time. Erica had a sickness that the doctors could not diagnose. She had suffered from this sickness for years. She saw the greatest specialists at UCLA and still had no answer. To us, the way her insides worked and did not work was a mystery, but to her Creator, there was no mystery. He knew all about her. Her body is still a mystery to people on earth. She has good days and bad days, but she has never lost God's perspective on her body. She reminds herself that God created her innermost being.

Maybe you, too, have an illness that the doctors do not know how to cure. God created your inward parts. He fashioned you. He knew that your body would work or not work. The words "inward parts" also could describe our personality. He made you to be exactly the way you are. He made you either extroverted or introverted. He made you love the stage or love to be behind the scenes. He made you good at math or not good at math but good at something else. He made no mistakes in you.

Maybe you do not like your personality. You think you are too shy or too loud. One of the harshest things someone ever said to me was that I was too loud. I was crushed and devastated. I vowed to use sign language for the rest of my days on earth. Finally, I came to the point when I just had to realize that God made me loud. He did not mess up or goof up. He is not in heaven saying, "Oops! Oh well, she'll just have to live with it." Our God, our Creator, is not like that. He made us the way He wanted us to be. In my case, that's loud.

> *Something deep inside us longs to be extraordinary and astonishing.*

You are fearfully made. In verse 14 we discover that we are "*fearfully*" made. In the Hebrew language, that word means a feeling of awe. You were made in awe.

Have you ever been in awe of something? When I moved to California, I drove my car out there. My parents came along, and we made a vacation out of the trip. As we passed through Arizona, we stopped at the Grand Canyon. The Grand Canyon is one of the natural wonders that I had always heard about, but I really couldn't imagine what it was like until I saw it. When I walked up to the edge of the canyon and looked across to the other rim, I was amazed. I stood in awe.

I picture God doing that with us. After He created us, He must have stepped back and stood in awe of His creation. You were fearfully [awesomely] made.

Then God's Word says *"wonderful"* are His works. The word *wonderful* means "separate, distinguished, extraordinary, or astonishing." Something deep inside us longs to be extraordinary and astonishing. The truth is that you are extraordinary! You are astonishing! God made you that way. Wonderful are His works! Wonderful are *you!*

Verse 15 says that your *"frame was not hidden"* from Him. Your frame is your body. What do you notice about a picture? The frame or the artwork? Why do people go to art galleries? Do they go to art galleries to look at the frames or the art inside those frames? No one goes to a gallery and stands in front of a painting and says, "Wow! Look at that frame. It is absolutely breathtaking!" They go to look at the art, of course!

To be honest with you, sometimes I tend to focus more on the frame than the art inside it. I used to want my frame (my body) to be considered "hot." Some of us dress provocatively in order to draw attention to our frame. But God is more concerned with our artwork (what's inside the frame). He wants that to be the attention grabber, not our body. Our artwork is made up of our character, our gifts, and our thoughts. This is what should draw people's attention.

Don't insult God. Verse 15 of Psalm 139 goes on to say that we were *"skillfully wrought."* One summer, I went to the Sawdust Art Festival in Laguna Beach and watched a man create a glass vase. He worked for over an hour on one vase, carefully molding the glass to be the exact shape he wanted. I couldn't help but picture God carefully and skillfully shaping me into what I have become today. He designed me short with a little nose, blue-green eyes, and blonde hair (OK, not all naturally blonde). Sometimes I tend to tell God that surely He made a mistake. At times I question God's skillful hand. I say, "I don't like my hips, my legs, my breasts, my bottom." But I had to realize that being displeased with my body and telling God that I wished I looked another way might be insulting to Him. I am basically telling God that He doesn't know what He is doing. Have you ever done that? Have I described you, too? If so, maybe you need to ask for God's forgiveness, and then thank Him for the way He created you. God did not mess up on you. You are His unique creation, one of His masterpieces. You are more priceless than that beautiful glass vase the artist designed. You are one of a kind and unique to God's purposes.

In verse 16 the psalmist says that God ordained your days on earth. The word *ordained* means that God established your lifetime and His purposes for your life. He has plans for you. Jeremiah 29:11 says, "'*For I know the plans that I have for you,' declares the* LORD, '*plans for welfare and not for calamity to give you a future and a hope.*'"

God gave you a unique shape. He has given you certain things that you love about yourself. He has given you unique experiences. He has given you a unique purpose. When God created you, He created you in His image. Genesis 1:27 says, "*God created man in His own image, in the image of God He created him; male and female He created them.*" You were uniquely created in the image of God. You were created to bear His likeness.

Finally we come to the last two verses of Psalm 139. The psalmist asks God to search him in order to see if there are any "*anxious thoughts*" in him. The psalmist is talking about your thoughts and more specifically about the things on which you meditate. When you are anxious about something, you think about it all the time. When you think about something nonstop, you are meditating on it. On what do you meditate? Being anxious means being pulled apart. Why are you anxious or pulled apart?

Are you meditating on your body or your personality? I cannot tell you how many times I still think about my body—some days more than others. Then I need to be like the psalmist and ask God if there is "*any hurtful way in me.*" To many of us, our body is our idol. Our image is our idol. It has become our way of life. Meditating on how much weight I need to lose used to be a way of life for me. My body was my idol. Ask God if your body has become your idol. Ask Him if you have chosen to worship His creation rather than Him, the Creator.

Learning How to Be Content

I hope you have caught a glimpse of what God thinks about you. I hope you can see the detail and thought that was behind creating you. God made you unique and extraordinary.

God is asking us to find contentment within ourselves. How do we become content with ourselves? The Bible says that contentment is learned. Paul wrote in Philippians 4:11, "*Not that I speak from want, for I have learned to be content in whatever circumstances I am.*"

How do you learn something? I played the piano for ten years. I took lessons every week and became very good. I loved playing the piano. In order to be good at something, such as playing the piano, practice is a must! I practiced the piano at least an hour a day. Some days I would practice for three hours! I practiced not only to get better, but also to memorize the songs. I think we need to practice being content with our bodies. The more we practice contentment, the more content we will be.

Ask God to give you a new perspective. The true secret of contentment is learning to see yourself through God's eyes. Contentment is something we must practice. Contentment is gaining the right perspective. God's Word promises that you can learn to be content and, like Paul, you can say "whatever you want, Lord." I am finally able to say with Paul that I have *learned* to be content in whatever circumstances I find myself. I have gained the right perspective on my body.

When you think about something nonstop, you are meditating on it.

While growing up, I went to my grandparents' house often. My grandfather would greet me the same way every time I went there. He would hug and kiss me. Then he'd call me beautiful and say, "One day you will be Miss America." He did this until he died. I was in high school then. His words troubled me for some time. I couldn't understand why he would think that about me. Was he just old and senile? (I was the one who had never had a date and who looked a little frumpy.) But no. My grandfather saw me through the eyes of love and pride. If my earthly grandfather saw me like Miss America, how does God see me? In order for me to see God's creation clearly, I needed better sight. I needed new glasses—new corrective lenses. In college, I finally saw the truth. I pray that you soon begin wearing spiritual glasses that will enable you to see yourself through God's eyes.

My battle with body image was heartbreaking. I lost control. I became addicted. The obsession to exercise was deeply guilt-producing and self-defeating. I knew God did not want me to live my life the way I was living it. I knew that this was not the kind of life that He intended for me. He wanted me to be free from the pain of seeing myself with eyes that were not trusting. He wanted me to be content with "Sarah."

Through the help of an accountability partner, I began the process of deliverance. It didn't happen overnight. It was a process. Finally, by my senior year of college—11 years after my problems first began, I had had enough. I sat on my bed and cried out to God saying, "I don't want to be controlled by this anymore." I cried it out over and over and over again. Every time I thought about it, I would surrender to God with the words, "I don't want to be controlled by it." Every time the thought entered my mind, I would command it to bow to the truth of God's Word. That's what God's Word tells us to do.

> *For though we walk in the flesh, we do not war according to the flesh, for the weapons of our warfare are not of the flesh, but divinely powerful for the destruction of fortresses. We are destroying speculations and every lofty thing raised up against the knowledge of God, and we are taking every thought captive to the obedience of Christ, and we are ready to punish all disobedience, whenever your obedience is complete.*
> —2 Corinthians 10:3–6

We are not fighting a physical battle; the battle we wage is in our minds. We are out to destroy any speculation or imagination that is not true. When you hear in your mind that you need to stop eating or you are not pretty enough, you need to recognize that is a lie. When lies come to your mind, you must replace them with truth. That is what it means to take every thought captive to the obedience of Jesus Christ. We must subject the lie to Christ. We must command the lie to listen to the truth of Christ, the truth that you are fearfully and wonderfully made. You are astonishing! You are extraordinary!

Learning contentment is an ongoing process. It does not happen overnight although I wish it did. When we practice contentment every day, we will begin to look at life differently. That's what I had to do. I had to allow God to change my mind and the way I thought. Then my life was changed. We need to think on things that are pleasing to God. Condemning thoughts about our body do not please God. Putting His creative work down does not please to Him.

I learned to love my body, God's creation. I learned an important word. I learned the word *moderation*. That was something I had never had in my life. I was either at the extreme of being obsessed with my body or at the extreme of doing nothing. Your body was created for physical activity, but being driven by exercise is not moderation. You are to take care of the body that God gave you by eating healthy, but being obsessed with every calorie is not moderation. I have found a life of moderation. By living in moderation, I am a smaller size than I was when I lived in obsession or neglect.

The Secret to Contentment

The secret to contentment and moderation is found in one word—worship. If you want to find contentment, you need to learn how to worship God with your body. First Corinthians 10:31 says, *"Whether, then, you eat or drink or whatever you do, do all to the glory of God."* Everything we do should be done for the glory of God. We should worship God in the way we eat. We should worship God in the way we exercise. God wants us to worship Him in everything—even our body! That's why Mark 12:30 says, *"and you shall love the LORD your God with all your heart, and with all your soul, and with all your mind, and with all your strength."*

Have you ever worshiped God with your body? Here's how I do it. I hate the treadmill, but I love to go for walks. So any chance I have, I walk outside. I usually walk on an oversized sidewalk in an area called the Alpharetta Greenway near Atlanta. This sidewalk runs alongside a creek and is covered with trees. I take my iPod and listen to worship songs. I have the most enjoyable experience singing praises to my Creator as I walk. Sometimes I scare the people I pass because I am singing out loud and they cannot hear the accompaniment I'm hearing through my headset!

I also enjoy Tae bo. Kicking and punching are great at relieving stress! Not too long ago, I was doing Tae bo in my basement and was praying while I kicked. I got so excited while praying that I began just jumping around and lifting up my hands. I got so caught up in praise that I neglected to do what Billy Blanks instructed me to do; I was too busy worshipping God with my body. Exercising can be a worship experience!

God Alone Is Worthy of Our Worship

When I think about worship, I think about respect. **God deserves our respect.** To really respect God, we must first understand why He deserves our respect. Many of us see little difference between man and God. We have a poor picture of who He is. When you realize that God is big and glorious and that we are little more than dust, we begin to get the picture. He is the Wondrous Creator of heaven and earth.

Respect is giving worth to God. It's saying, "God, You matter to me," Only God is worthy of our worship. You see people who idolize, chase after, or follow things other than God. You can see how their lives lack the meaning that believing God gives. We must be careful to give God worth, rather than to give our bodies worth. Rather than chase after a dream of looking a certain way, we need to chase after God.

Can you name any of the Ten Commandments? How about the very first commandment? When God gave the Ten Commandments, it was as if He were saying, "The very first thing I want you to know is, *'You shall have no other gods before Me'*" (Exodus 20:3). Now why would He make that the *first* commandment? Because only God is worthy of our worship and because He knows our tendency to put other things above Him. In a psalm of thanks to the Lord recorded in 1 Chronicles 16:25, King David proclaimed, *"For great is the LORD and most worthy of praise"* (NIV).

> *Even though I have gained control over my body image problem and all that goes with it, I still must give it to God continually.*

Nothing else is more worthy of our praise than God—certainly not our bodies. Some of us worship our body as if it were a god. But to worship anything else is to set up an idol—a rival to our Creator. Is your body a rival to God?

How do we know if we have stopped worshiping God and started worshiping our bodies? I'll give you a little test. How do you spend most of your time? Do you spend a lot of time thinking about and taking care of your body? How much time do you spend thinking about what you should eat or what you ate? How much time do you spend exercising? The amount of time you spend on something shows how much value you put on it. When you value something, you honor it with your time. So if you spend a lot of time taking care of and thinking about your body, you are worshiping it rather than God. Your body has become your idol, and God's Word commands that we put no idol before Him.

Not only are we to worship God by our respect, but **we worship Him also by being single-minded.** Second Corinthians 11:3 says, *"But I am* *afraid that just as Eve was deceived by the serpent's cunning, your minds may somehow be led astray from your sincere and pure devotion to Christ"* (NIV). This verse says that you need to be single-minded in your devotion to Christ.

One of our spiritual problems is that we are easily distracted. It's as if we all have spiritual attention deficit disorder. We have trouble concentrating on God. The culture we live in bombards us with a million things to think about...things on which to focus our attention. Our TVs have hundreds of channels. We have Internet access to the whole world. We have cell phones that enable us to reach anybody, anytime. We have to work at paying attention to anything. And we have to work at paying attention to Christ. Single-minded Christians pay attention to God, to His commands, to who He is, and to His ways.

I no longer am caught in the deadly trap of self-worship, but I certainly was. Sometimes even now, those thoughts creep back into my mind. When they do, I immediately surrender them to God. Even though I have gained control over my body image problem and all that goes with it, I still must give it to God continually. I have to learn to be content with *me* every day. Each day I must make the choice of whether I am going to be *out of control* or I am going to let God be *in control*.

Whenever Satan tries to deceive me with his lies, such as "You're not pretty enough" or "You're not thin enough" or "You're not worthy of love," I quote God's Word as truth: "Psalm 139:14 says, *'I will give thanks to [God] for I am fearfully and wonderfully made.'"* God made me exactly the way I am, and He makes no mistake. You do not have to look for satisfaction from anyone other than God, because He is satisfied with you. Ask Him to give you His perspective, His glasses, to wear.

Not Self-Worship, but Self-Worth

Our culture says that externals are what establish our self-worth. The world says that what we do plus what others think of us equals our self-worth. But God says that it's all about internals. God says that who He is plus what He thinks of us equals our self-worth. He establishes our self-worth. God thinks amazing things about you. After all, you are His creation, His masterpiece.

While we are not to worship our own bodies, I have learned that if I don't love myself, I can't love others. God used me when I was out of control and when I believed lies, but I must admit, I wasn't an effective Christian. Being content deep in my soul has freed me to accept myself the way I am. And when we accept ourselves and are content, we are able to love others. God loves you. He created you. He accepts you. **So accept yourself, let God love you, and then you can love others.**

The Godly Woman

What kind of woman do you hope to be? A woman without self-control who is obsessed with the way she looks? A woman who is never content with herself? Not me. There are several women in the Bible whom I would like to emulate. God promises that you can be a woman of contentment. What does a godly woman look like? In Proverbs 31:29–31, the description of a godly woman is provided: *"Many daughters have done nobly, but you excel them all. Charm is deceitful and beauty is vain, but a woman who fears the LORD, she shall be praised. Give her the product of her hands, and let her works praise her in the gates."* The woman who fears the Lord is praised for her character. According to the dictionary, character means "the set of qualities that make somebody distinctive." It's the qualities that make somebody interesting or attractive. It's moral strength and reputation. Contentment is part of the godly woman's character package.

Contentment is learned. It comes through practice. Contentment is the result of faith. You can begin today to walk towards contentment. It is a process that promises to bring peace, joy, and satisfaction.

I challenge you to examine your heart. Is your self-worth based on externals, or is it based on what God's says about you? What difference would it make in your life and relationships if you accepted and lived God's truth found in Psalm 139? Contentment is a godly characteristic. Begin today looking at yourself through God's eyes. Start your journey to contentment today. Join the apostle Paul in saying, "Not that I speak from want; for I have learned to be content in whatever circumstances I am." Be loved, be satisfied, and revel in who you are. God made you wonderfully unique. Be content to be who you are and worship the Creator and not the creation.

Bible Study Questions

1 Memorize Psalm 139:14. Write it down on a card and carry it with you this week.

2 What does it mean to be content? Based on your definition, are you content with you?

3 What do you think is the opposite of contentment?

4 Read Matthew 6:25–34. How many times does this passage mention anxious thoughts?

5 How much of your day is spent worrying about things you can't control, for example, the length of your legs or the size of your nose?

6 Read Psalm 90:14; Psalm 145:16, 19; Psalm 65:4; Psalm 103:5; Matthew 5:6; and 1 Timothy 6:6. What do these verses have in common?

7 God wants to satisfy you, and He is satisfied with you. You are a child of God. Write about your state of contentment. Where are you and what do you need?

Body. Beauty. Boys.

Write your reactions to Sarah's thoughts in this chapter. Which thoughts relate to you? Which ones don't relate to you? How did you feel as you read?

_____

_____

_____

_____

_____

_____

_____

_____

_____

_____

_____

_____

_____

_____

_____

_____

CHAPTER SIX

Accountability: Having a Friend and Being a Friend

When I was in middle school, I was best friends with two girls. Brandi, Sandi, and I were cheerleaders. We did everything together. We dressed alike and acted alike. We were inseparable. During our first year of high school, we decided to try out for cheerleading together. Cheerleading had become the biggest thing in our lives. During the tryouts, something tragic happened. I went up for a jump and landed on the side of my ankle. I can still remember hobbling to the side of the gym. At the end of the tryouts, all the girls lined up and awaited their fate. I heard the names of Brandi and Sandi called. I waited hopefully, but my name was never called. I was devastated. I felt as though my life had come to a complete stop. I walked to my mom's car and crawled into the front seat, utterly dejected. I curled up into a fetal position and cried all the way home.

My life took a major turn that day. Over the next year, Brandi and Sandi made new friends and became popular. Our friendship dropped to a level of merely acquaintance. My faith, however, grew stronger than ever before because I had to learn to lean on my friend Jesus. I gained a valuable lesson from that experience.

The Importance of Friends

In our culture, we are under a lot of influences. We are influenced by the media, our parents, and our friends, to name just a few. Studies have shown that friends are the biggest influence in the lives of students today.

If that statement is true, then this principle is true: Your friendships help determine the choices you make.

God designed us to be in relationships and involved in others' lives. It's difficult to choose the right friends. It's not like *The Bachelorette*, a TV show in which a woman's odds of finding a boyfriend are 25 to 1. The goal for the end of the show is that one woman leaves with her best friend and soul mate. That is absolutely ludicrous. You can't find a soul mate in an hour. However, the show does tell us that people want to have deep and lasting friendships.

The Bible says that deep friendships equal a better life. Ecclesiastes 4:9 says, *"Two are better than one because they have a good return for their labor."* I've seen in real life how much better two can be than one. When speaking to students, I've seen girls with sad faces waiting in the front of the church for the service to begin. As soon as a friend arrives, their faces brighten. Our lives are enriched by our friends.

To Help, Friends Must Be Real

Girls who battle eating disorders need friendships, but often don't form them because they are ashamed or embarrassed. Many such girls just do not believe they have a problem and, therefore, refuse help. It might be difficult to be a friend to someone who cannot see clearly. So how do you help someone who doesn't want to be helped?

Always begin by developing a simple, sincere friendship with them. This is not a project; this is a person. Don't start right away with any "helping agenda" you might have. If you aren't willing to have a *real* friendship with this person, don't initiate a false one—it might be more damaging in the long run.

If you have concerns about any peer, whether you are able to help the person yourself or not, be sure that a trusted adult is aware of the problem and available to help that peer. Express your concerns to a school counselor, teacher, youth minister, the person's parents, or some other trusted adult. If the adult you talk with is unwilling to address the concern, you might try to speak to some other adult on the list. Getting someone needed help is important if you can't offer it yourself.

As you begin to help someone with whom you have a caring friendship, get ready for some difficult, but ultimately rewarding, situations. Be ready to be put off, laughed at, or snubbed before the person accepts her problem.

Ask God to guide you as you reach out. Always begin from a position of real friendship, and be sure the person knows you care for her as a friend.

Real Friends Speak the Truth in Love

The first thing you can do to help this hurting friend is to speak the truth in love (Ephesians 4:15). Proverbs 24:26 (CEV) says, *"Giving an honest answer is a sign of true friendship."* It's tough to be honest about such a delicate situation. It's difficult to speak the truth when you know the other person will become angry with you for what you say.

I have a friend who confided in me about her body image struggles. I prayed for her and asked about her struggle on a weekly basis. After some time, she began to struggle even more. She pushed me away. I can remember how much I hurt for her, but I was afraid to confront her any more. I talked to my mentor about the situation. She said, "It sounds as if you care more about the friendship, than the friend." She was right. I didn't want to ruin an already strained relationship. I was afraid that if I spoke the truth, we would never be friends again. But if you and I truly care for a friend who is hurting, we will speak the truth even if it costs us the relationship.

Real Friends Hold Each Other Accountable

The second step in helping a hurting friend is to hold her accountable. Proverbs 27:17 says, *"Iron sharpens iron, so one man sharpens another."* Friends sharpen each other, keep each other focused, make each other better. Let's revisit the biblical principle that *"two are better than one"* mentioned earlier in this chapter.

> *Two are better than one because they have a good return for their labor. For if either of them falls, the one will lift up his companion. But woe to the one who falls when there is not another to lift him up. Furthermore, if two lie down together they keep warm, but how can one be warm alone? And if one can overpower him who is alone, two can resist him. A cord of three strands is not quickly torn apart.*
> —Ecclesiastes 4:9–12

If one falls, then another is there to pick him up. If your friend falls, you are there to lift her off the floor.

My best friend, Lisa, is my accountability partner. Lisa has also struggled with body image, so we know the signs in each other. The battle with body image is a selfish fight because we focus all our attention on ourselves. We cannot fight this battle alone. When I was struggling to overcome my problem, she would ask me how I was doing with my body image. She would ask me whether I was walking in freedom or bondage. We agreed to pray for the other whenever false thoughts rose in our own minds. Each time as I began to pray for Lisa in response to false thoughts that were cropping up in my mind, my focus was taken off my own need and placed on hers, although I didn't even know whether she was struggling that day. It helped me to know that I had a friend who was praying for me even when I was not strong enough to pray, and it helped me to have a friend to pray for on those days that I so desperately needed to get my mind off myself.

> *It helped me to know that I had a friend who was praying for me…and it helped me to have a friend to pray for on those days that I so desperately needed to get my mind off myself.*

Accountability is really only possible when you develop quality friendships. Your best option for an accountability partner is someone with whom you already have a deep, caring friendship. Accountability involves both sides of the friendship coin—*needing* a friend and *being* a friend. Since I have experience being in both of those situations, I share from both perspectives. Accountability adds insight to decisions, truth to perception, and hope in times of hurting.

Accountability adds insight to decisions. First of all, having a friend who will hold you accountable can add insight into your decisions. Proverbs 12:15 says, "The way of a fool is right in his own eyes, but a wise man is he who listens to counsel." Choosing to make the right decision about what to eat or how much to exercise can become difficult when you are in the middle of the fight. The problem with body image is that you cannot see yourself clearly. You cannot see the truth about God's creation. Having a friend who holds you accountable can add insight into the wise choice to make.

Accountability adds truth to perception. An accountability partner also can bring truth to your perception. She brings perspective to your situation. When you are in the battle, sometimes you are too immersed to sense what is really true.

It's strange that I can see my friends so clearly but have a hard time seeing myself clearly. I know that my accountability partner sees me clearly, and she also sees God's Word clearly. Her job is to bring truth to my skewed perception.

Accountability brings hope in times of hurting. Finally, an accountability partner can bring hope in times of hurting. Hope brings healing. It helps to know that you are not alone. It helps to know there is someone nearby to help you through the rough times. During the rough times, Satan may try to hold you captive by deception through his lies and the lies you tell others. Confessing those lies brings freedom. Whenever I go to Lisa with my struggles, she listens to my confession. When I am truthful, I find freedom.

> *Therefore, confess your sins to one another, and pray for one another so that you may be healed. The effective prayer of a righteous man can accomplish much.*
> —James 5:16

Quality Friendships

God promises you friendship. He keeps His promise through Jesus who is a Friend who will stick closer to you than a brother (Proverbs 18:24). God also desires that you be wise when it comes to choosing friends. Psalm 91:4 says, "*His faithful promises are your armor and protection*" (NLT). May His promises protect you in your friendships.

This section about friendship is important for any young woman struggling with body image problems. These problems are so prevalent among girls in middle school, high school, and college that it's likely to affect several girls in any group of friends. You, the reader, and any friend you are trying to help can benefit immensely by developing quality friendships. To develop quality friendships, start by being choosy. You must be careful about who you take into your confidence. Be friendly with everyone, but close friend with few.

I knew a lot of people in high school. I was popular, not because I partied, but because I was friendly to everyone. I was voted Most Dependable my senior year. I'm not bragging about that. I was actually disappointed, because at the time, I wanted to be remembered for something else. Dependability seemed so boring, but now I realize that I like being remembered for that quality. Even though I knew a lot of people, my high school years were lonely. I didn't have many close friends—friends who really clicked with me and understood me. My mom prayed for years and years that I would have friends of a kindred spirit. It didn't happen until college.

We need to surround ourselves with friends who will encourage us and speak truth into our circumstances. We need to be **choosy** about our close friends. They will shape our life.

Not only do we need to be choosy, but we need to *be* the type of friend we want to *have*. We need to be positive with others. We need to encourage them. If you want encouragement *from* someone, give encouragement *to* someone. Proverbs 27:2 says, *"Let another praise you, and not your own mouth; a stranger, and not your own lips."* Look outside yourself. Take an interest in the lives of others. Build up others with your words. People love to be asked about what's going on in their lives. Ask them. It shows you care; it shows you are interested in them.

> *We need to surround ourselves with friends who will encourage us and speak truth into our circumstances.*

To develop quality friendships, be unique by keeping confidentiality. Proverbs 11:13 says, *"He who goes about as a talebearer reveals secrets, but he who is trustworthy conceals a matter."* Be trustworthy. When someone tells you something in confidence, be true to her. Respect her. The only time to break confidence is when the information that person tells you is going to hurt someone else or the person talking. Then you need to tell someone who can help.

Even if you don't have friends, you have a Friend who sticks closer than a brother. God promises you friendship. God wants you to be His friend. God created you to have a relationship with Him. Until we develop a relationship with Him, we will never be fully satisfied. Let Him meet your deepest need. Learn how to develop quality friendships and most importantly develop your friendship with God.

Kelley's Story

An eating disorder can be very painful, not only for the girl who suffers from it, but also for her friends and family. At the church where I serve as

Girls' Minister, one student, Kelley, had an eating disorder for about two and a half years. It wasn't until six or seven months into it that she was "discovered." Her mom and dad immediately took her to therapy, where she was encouraged to talk about her feelings, and where she learned how to admit she had an eating disorder.

At first, Kelley was scared because she didn't know how to approach the subject or what to say. Greater than those fears, however, were her fears of how her friends might react. Her very best friend was shocked. She had no idea about Kelley's struggles! But she became the one friend Kelley could count on, trust, and use as a sounding board. Kelley was able to tell her friend when she was struggling with her eating disorder a particular day or week and when she needed a shoulder to cry on. Her friend was always there for her.

In my opinion, one of the worst things a friend or parent can do to someone with an eating disorder is to over-analyze how they eat or don't eat.

Since Kelley's therapist was the person who held her accountable each week by asking her how her eating had been, that left her best friend free to just be a friend.

About four other girlfriends also ended up knowing Kelley's story. Some learned of it because she told them. Others found out because she told of her struggle as a part of her testimony of how God had helped her. Two friends in particular did not respond as well as she had hoped. They began to overanalyze her eating behavior. (In my opinion, one of the worst things a friend or parent can do to someone with an eating disorder is to overanalyze how they eat or don't eat. It's not the observer's responsibility to be the food police.)

Friends and family who knew of her struggles sometimes tried to encourage her by making positive comments about her looks. Kelley told me that she would rather have heard loving, sincere comments about how much friends and family enjoyed her presence or how nice it was to see her smiling that day. Most girls with eating disorders whom I have known don't want to be told, "You look so good!" If the girl is still in a negative mindset, she will most likely interpret "You look good" as "You've gained weight; you look bigger."

I asked Kelley what she would want friends of a person with an eating disorder to know. She said, "My advice for friends who know someone with an eating disorder is to first make sure the girl's parents or some other trusted adult knows. Once that is clear, friends should be aware of the eating disordered person's insecurities, fears, worries, and apprehensions toward food in any situation. Encouraging the girl to participate in weekend activities, inviting her out but not forcing her to dinners, finding out what the girl feels most comfortable doing, and listening to each conversation with your whole attention are all great things for friends to focus on. It is always best *not* to focus on what she is eating or not eating. Let her work that out with her nutritionist and personal therapist."

Throughout Kelley's experience, God played a huge role. In the beginning, Kelley was angry at God, but prayed to Him at the same time to take the pain and obsession away. Even though she prayed, she never fully gave up her control issues—not until she was at her lowest possible point. Her lowest point was when she realized that she could not be normal around her friends, she blacked out while running her daily punishment, and she finally saw the hurt in her mother's eyes as she gazed upon Kelley's frail body. It was then that she relinquished control.

After becoming broken, empty, and helpless, she prayed that God would forgive her and that He would show her how to take care of her body again. From that point on, she gradually learned to eat in a way that glorified God by not eating too little and by not eating too much. During this transitional phase, having a mentor within the church helped her enormously.

Importance of Godly Counsel

In the midst of my struggles, I was blessed to have a Christian mentor. My own mentor was able to point out to me what the Bible says about our bodies and food and other concerns, whereas my therapist didn't bring up God at all. Some girls who struggle extensively with actual eating disorders need to experience therapy. As for me in my battle with a poor body image, I needed care from a mentor and an accountability partner. Having someone, whether it's a spiritually mature friend or a mentor, to pray for you and love you unconditionally is immensely helpful in the healing process.

Throughout my own battle with body image, I was honest with my accountability partner, and I was also honest with a trusted adult who was not my mentor. One reason why God has put people in our lives is to give us counsel about our decisions. There is value in going to other believers for advice. We are often too close to our own situation to see all the details. Emotions can cloud our judgment. The Book of Proverbs in the Bible says a lot about seeking counsel:

> A wise man will hear and increase in learning,
> And a man of understanding will acquire wise counsel.
> —Proverbs 1:5

> The way of a fool is right in his own eyes,
> But a wise man is he who listens to counsel.
> —Proverbs 12:15

> Through insolence comes nothing but strife,
> But wisdom is with those who receive counsel.
> —Proverbs 13:10

> Oil and perfume make the heart glad,
> So a man's counsel is sweet to his friend.
> —Proverbs 27:9

First Kings 12 is the account of a would-be king who seemed to realize the importance of seeking counsel, but not the importance of the counsel being godly counsel.

Let me give you a little background before we get into that particular story. Saul was the first king of Israel, and although he started out doing right, he soon turned bad. Then came David who was a good king—a man after God's own heart. David's son Solomon, who succeeded him as king, became well known for his wisdom. Solomon was good early in life, but he later started making wrong choices. God told Solomon that his kingdom was going to be divided after he died, and He determined that Jeroboam, who was not even in line to be king, was going to rule over Israel.

When Solomon died, everyone assumed that his son Rehoboam would be king. Jeroboam and the people of Israel came to Rehoboam and said that if he made their heavy yoke lighter, they would serve him. Rehoboam asked for some time to seek counsel before making a decision:

Then [Rehoboam] said to them, "Depart for three days, then return to me." So the people departed.

King Rehoboam consulted with the elders who had served his father Solomon while he was still alive, saying, "How do you counsel me to answer this people?"

Then they spoke to him, saying, "If you will be a servant to this people today, and will serve them and grant them their petition, and speak good words to them, then they will be your servants forever."

But he forsook the counsel of the elders which they had given him, and consulted with the young men who grew up with him and served him. So he said to them, "What counsel do you give that we may answer this people who have spoken to me, saying, 'Lighten the yoke which your father put on us'?"

The young men who grew up with him spoke to him, saying, "Thus you shall say to this people who spoke to you, saying, 'Your father made our yoke heavy, now you make it lighter for us!' But you shall speak to them, 'My little finger is thicker than my father's loins! Whereas my father loaded you with a heavy yoke, I will add to your yoke.'"

—1 Kings 12:5–11

Rehoboam first consulted with experienced elders who provided advice that agreed with one of Solomon's wise proverbs: "*A gentle answer turns away wrath, but a harsh word stirs up anger*" (Proverbs 15:1). But then he made a huge mistake. He chose to listen to his friends who did not speak truth to him. His friends gave him poor advice. Their advice was contrary to God's Word, God's truth, and God's nature. We can learn from Rehoboam's mistake. We need to be choosy about whom we go to for advice. If you are the hurting friend, choose wisely whom you listen to, and if you are the friend who helps, make sure to give wise counsel—counsel that can be supported by God's Word, His truth.

Another Sarah's Story

In the summer of 2003, I met a young woman named Sarah who was a junior in high school. She was a regular attendee of my weekly girls'

Bible study. Week after week, I noticed she had some warning signs of blurred vision. One night before Bible study, she excused herself to go to the restroom, and I followed her. When I walked through the door, I could tell that I had foiled her plan of throwing up what she had just eaten. While we were in the restroom, I confronted Sarah with my concern about her eating problem. She was shocked that I would confront her. She looked at me, and her eyes told me she was wondering whether I could possibly understand. At first, she denied her problem. She used the same excuses she had given everyone else. I told her that I would like to meet with her some time apart from the Bible study.

We began to meet on a weekly basis, and she began to trust me. It took her a long time to realize what God was doing by placing me in her life. I wanted her to see that I was not there to pass judgment or give her a quick fix. I wanted to be someone who pointed Sarah to truth. After weeks of meeting, she finally opened up: she came to one of our scheduled meetings, sat down, and poured out her entire story. When she was finished, I could tell that she was waiting for me to yell or leave the room. Instead, I got up out of my chair and hugged her. When you are in the midst of such pain and darkness, a hug from a trusted mentor who cares is priceless.

From that day on, things began to get better for her. We began to meet about twice a week to talk about our lives and, in particular, the progress she had made with her eating disorder. There were weeks when she reported struggling and slipping back into believing in lies. She would sit down with me ready to tell me a predetermined lie. However, when it got down to the actual lying, she knew God wanted her to be open and honest. As her mentor, my job was simply to listen, care, and speak God's truth into her life. Through my help as a mentor, she was able to submit her obsession to God and walk in truth. Sarah was able to learn to give God control of her eating and exercise habits.

> *When I walked through the door, I could tell that I had foiled her plan of throwing up what she had just eaten. While we were in the restroom, I confronted Sarah with my concern about her eating problem. She was shocked that I would confront her. She looked at me, and her eyes told me she was wondering whether I could possibly understand.*

Action and Compassion

As a friend, how do you care for someone who is hurting? What does care look like? I've chosen two words to describe it: *action and compassion*.

Action is where you express more than just words. Let's say that one of your friends shows up and admits she is hurting because she cannot see herself clearly. Do you say, "Oh, I'm sorry to hear that!" and walk away? Someone who really cares says, "I'm going to take action. I'm going to do more than just say, 'I'm sorry to hear that.' I'm going to figure out how I can care for you." Take action by being there for her. Take action by writing encouraging notes to her. Take action by praying for her.

You can also show you care by having compassion. Compassion means that you hurt when she hurts. Just listening is an expression of care. Compassion happens when you look into somebody's eyes, and you can see a reflection of the pain that you have felt at some time in your life. Eyes communicate. Compassion shows in the eyes of the caring person.

Two kinds of listening are possible: *actual listening* and *fake listening*. Some of us have mastered the art of fake listening. How often does it happen that you are hearing someone talk, but you're not actually listening in detail to what that person is saying? One adult in my life turned out to be a fake listener. She was a nice lady, and a lot of people admired all her accomplishments, but she was the kind of person who didn't hear what I said when I talked. She wanted me to believe she cared, but she didn't. I could tell that by her eyes and actions. She had no empathy. Real compassion involves actual listening.

When you find people who are truly listening, you want to talk to them even more. You want to open your innermost heart to them. Actual listening is a picture of caring. Your hurting friend needs compassion. When a person really cares—truly has compassion—he or she will remove the word "convenient" from their vocabulary. Caring is not a matter of convenience. Caring is not always easy.

Sometimes you may feel inadequate to help a friend if you have never struggled with the thing with which they are struggling. But you still can help. My friend Alyssa has never struggled with body image the way I have. Yet she has learned what it means to be a friend to someone who has.

She first learned that it is important not to speak a bunch of cheesy lines to make her feel like a good friend while doing nothing. The hurts of those who struggle with body image are not something that can be healed by a "fix-it-all" line. She learned this truth because one of her hurting friends was honest enough to tell her that directly. It can be very hard at times not to just start spouting words in an attempt to "fix" your friend. Trying to fix her is actually hurtful. No one wants to be commanded all the time to simply eat more or stop what they are doing. Some honest souls told Alyssa that when they are constantly asked about how much they have eaten in a day, it makes them want to eat less.

The second thing Alyssa learned was to encourage her friends to attend a support group where they can connect with other people struggling with the same things. Sometimes *we* want to be the one who fixes a problem, but in reality, persons with eating disorders may need more than you can offer. People who are going through the same things are better able to support one another and hold each other accountable.

Most importantly, pray for your hurting friend. Sometimes it's easy to forget that prayer is powerful. Sometimes we feel as though prayer is not enough. But prayer is of great value in changing circumstances. Pray for your friends and have faith that God is hearing and answering your prayers. The one thing Alyssa's friends have all continued to tell her is that her prayers for them mean more than anything else she could possibly do or say.

Jesus, the Greatest Friend

How can you be a friend to someone who hurts? We have an example to follow. There is someone who was and is the greatest Friend to the weak. Learn from Jesus. Matthew 26 tells of a time when Jesus, Himself, was hurting. We can learn from this account the kind of help He sought.

> Then Jesus went with his disciples to a place called Gethsemane, and he said to them, "Sit here while I go over there and pray." He took Peter and the two sons of Zebedee along with him, and he began to be sorrowful and troubled. Then he said to them, "My soul is overwhelmed with sorrow to the point of death. Stay here and keep watch with me."
>
> Going a little farther, he fell with his face to the ground and prayed, "My Father, if it is possible, may this cup be taken from me. Yet not as I will, but as you will."

*Then he returned to his disciples and found them sleeping.
"Could you men not keep watch with me for one hour?" he
asked Peter. "Watch and pray so that you will not fall into
temptation. The spirit is willing, but the body is weak."*

*He went away a second time and prayed, "My Father, if
it is not possible for this cup to be taken away unless I drink
it, may your will be done."*

*When he came back, he again found them sleeping,
because their eyes were heavy. So he left them and went away
once more and prayed the third time, saying the same thing.*

*Then he returned to the disciples and said to them, "Are
you still sleeping and resting? Look, the hour is near, and the
Son of Man is betrayed into the hands of sinners. Rise, let us
go! Here comes my betrayer!"*
—Matthew 26:36–46 (NIV)

When Jesus knew He had been betrayed, the first thing He did was to grab three of His disciples to go pray with Him. He told them His need. He said, *"My soul is overwhelmed with sorrow to the point of death. Stay here and keep watch with me."* Then He went off to pray. He came back three times. I don't think He came back to check up on the disciples and make sure they were watching or praying; I think Jesus wanted their company. He needed their support. He was about to face the most difficult experience of His life. He was about to face the cross. What Jesus needed was someone to be there for Him. He needed someone to whom He could verbalize His pain. Jesus knew He was about to die. He was about to face the sin of the world and condemnation from the Father. He knew He should not try to mourn alone. He took three friends with Him for support. He let His friends be His friends.

Honesty Before God

Your friend may have never had an opportunity to verbalize what's in her heart. For years, I tried to deny my heartache and act like I wasn't really hurting, but I was. I thought that keeping my pain stuffed inside would make things better, but it only made things worse. My hurt eventually made itself apparent. As we allow our friends to verbalize their pain to us, we can also encourage them to verbalize their pain to God. Most people aren't honest with God. In prayer, they say nice things to God and even about God, but they have so much hurt and rage toward Him that they are too terrified to admit it out loud; they are really suffering. Instead, they pretend that they are not hurt and angry toward God. Maybe they think God cannot handle their heartache. Maybe they think God will be mad at them. But God is not like that. It is impossible for God not to care about us. God knows when we are mad and hurting. And when we finally tell Him, we are just telling God something He already knows.

Psalm 62:8 says, *"Trust in Him at all times, O people; pour out your heart before Him; God is a refuge for us."* The words *"pour out"* mean "to bare your soul"—bare your soul through tears or complaints. God desires us to be honest with Him about the pain in our lives. Encourage your hurting friend to pour out her heart to God. Jesus said, *"if it is possible, may this cup be taken from me."* Jesus spoke honestly when He addressed the heavenly Father. It is possible for us to get angry at God, cry with God, and yet honestly express our feelings to Him.

> *Listen to my cry for help, my King and my God, for to you*
> *I pray. In the morning, O LORD, you hear my voice; in the*
> *morning I lay my requests before you and wait in expectation.*
> —Psalm 5:2–3 (NIV)

To be a friend to someone who cannot see herself clearly, encourage her to crawl up in God's lap and speak honestly to Him. Encourage her to wait in expectation for what God wants to offer. What He offers is freedom and hope.

Bible Study Questions

1 Memorize Ecclesiastes 4:9. Write it down on a card and carry it with you this week.

2 What are the top five qualities you want in a friend?

3 Are your current friendships meeting that standard?

4 Read Proverbs 24:26 and Proverbs 17:17. Do you have a friend like this?

5 Read 1 Samuel 18:1. What do you think caused Jonathan to become "*one in spirit*" with David? What do you think that means?

6 Do you have a friend with whom you feel "*one in spirit*"? Explain.

7 This week, pray about who can be either an accountability partner to you or a spiritual mentor.

Body, Beauty, Boys.

Write your reactions to Sarah's thoughts in this chapter. Which thoughts relate to you? Which ones don't relate to you? How did you feel as you read?

_____

_____

_____

_____

_____

_____

_____

_____

_____

_____

_____

_____

_____

_____

_____

_____

CHAPTER SEVEN

God Wants to Use Your Past

Most of the girls I have counseled about body image issues feel ashamed and useless. But that kind of thinking couldn't be further from the truth. You are valued by the Creator. When God forgives you, He gives you a brand new start. He does not hold a grudge against you for your sin. He makes you a new person. The old has gone and the new has come. In Christ, there is no reason to feel ashamed, but the enemy we fight wants you to feel ashamed. His job is to deceive you and then make you feel ashamed and unworthy. But God can turn your story of overcoming pain in your past into someone else's hope for the future.

The first time I shared my testimony about my past struggles with body image was to about 200 junior high students. I was scared to death. I had often been in front of crowds either singing or playing the piano, but never to share my past and the secrets that had held me in bondage for years. I was a junior in college when I spoke to those students, and I was still struggling with my body image issues. I battled this disorder intensely for another year after this speech. Could God really use me if I was not 100 percent free from my disorder?

I can still remember the faces of the students as I looked out over the podium. I began to tell my story. With every word, I could feel a link in a chain breaking within me. It was freeing to stand up and tell others what God had done in my life. It was freeing to tell others about the foolish choices I had made. It was freeing to tell others the lies I had believed. I was telling them so that they would know the truth.

Advertise the Truth

I believe that God used my story that day, even though I still had a long way to go with my own issues. When you begin to speak the truth, it takes away the power of the lies. With every breath, as I told what God had done, lies began to shatter. I no longer felt ashamed of my story. I saw, firsthand, how God wanted to use my past.

> *When you begin to speak the truth, it takes away the power of the lies.*

I now travel across the world telling everyone what God has done. The book you are reading now is a testimony of God's grace as I began to be obedient and to share my story. I have realized that even if I help only one person with my story, my struggle has been worth it. It's been worth fighting this battle. It's been worth all the struggles. It's been worth all the pain. It's been worth everything if it comforts just one person and helps lead her to truth.

Someone needs to hear your story, too. God wants to reach someone through you. Just let God do His work in you; then let Him use your past to help others. To comfort others, we must first be comforted ourselves.

> *Blessed be the God and Father of our Lord Jesus Christ, the Father of mercies and God of all comfort, who comforts us in all our affliction so that we will be able to comfort those who are in any affliction with the comfort with which we ourselves are comforted by God. For just as the sufferings of Christ are ours in abundance, so also our comfort is abundant through Christ. But if we are afflicted, it is for your comfort and salvation; or if we are comforted, it is for your comfort, which is effective in the patient enduring of the same sufferings which we also suffer; and our hope for you is firmly grounded, knowing that as you are sharers of our sufferings, so also you are sharers of our comfort.*
> —2 Corinthians 1:3–7

The God of all comfort is ready to comfort you so that you can comfort someone else. One of my favorite things to do is to sit across from a young woman and, after sharing my story, hear her freely admit her struggles. The God of all comfort is working! The Greek verb for *comfort* means "to call to one's side, therefore, to aid." The God of all comfort comes to your side to encourage you and give you aid so that you can go to another's side and comfort her. I find that extremely motivating.

Second Corinthians 1:5 says that *"our comfort is abundant through Christ."* The word *abundant* means great plenty, more than needed. The comfort of God is that way for us. He knows what we need and gives us more than we need.

Keep Standing in Grace

God's comfort is a gift of His magnificent grace. We learned in an earlier chapter that grace is God's unmerited favor toward us. Galatians 5:1 says, *"It is for freedom that Christ has set us free. Stand firm, then, and do not let yourselves be burdened again by a yoke of slavery"* (NIV). Christ came to set us free. God's grace towards us through Christ is for freedom. We need to stand firm in this freedom.

There is a truth about grace that I want you to understand so that you will understand why God can use your past. The truth about grace is that you have total access to it. Romans 5:1–2 teaches us: *"Therefore, having been justified by faith, we have peace with God through our Lord Jesus Christ, through whom also we have obtained our introduction by faith into this grace in which we stand; and we exult in hope of the glory of God."*

The verb *stand* in the statement *"in which we stand"* is in the perfect tense. In Greek, the perfect tense indicates that it is an action that took place in the past but continues to be true in the present. At salvation you and I were not only given access to the grace of God for that particular moment, but we stand in that grace right now. Having access to the grace of God means that everything Jesus Christ is and everything He has is available to us. So when you encounter difficult circumstances, such as dealing with your discontentment or telling others your story, you have access to His grace.

When I lived in California, I met and became friends with the members of the band Switchfoot. The good thing about having friends who are in a band is that you get to see them on a regular basis, even if you live across the country. Even though I moved to Atlanta, Georgia, I saw this band a couple of times a year. At every concert, they would hand me an all-access pass. I loved this pass because I could go anywhere in the concert facilities. All I had to do was show my pass to the security guards.

I had such freedom. That's the way it is with God's grace. He has given us an all-access pass to His grace. At any moment when you feel weak, show your all-access pass. When you need to share your story and you're afraid, show your all-access pass. When you feel far from God, His grace is available. When you can't say no, His grace is available. When you hear lies, His grace is available. Whatever it looks like to you, His grace is available. Not only is God's grace available, but it is also sufficient.

> "My grace is sufficient for you, for my power is made perfect in weakness." Therefore I will boast all the more gladly about my weaknesses, so that Christ's power may rest on me.
> —2 Corinthians 12:9 (NIV)

Christ's power is made perfect in weakness. When you give your weakness to Christ, He gives you His strength and power. His power rests on us. That's why Paul encouraged us in these verses to boast about weakness; it is then that we are able to rely on God's power. The more we rely on God's power, the more freedom we experience. God's grace brings about freedom.

Our responsibility is to simply ask for His grace. Faith is what activates grace. Ephesians 2:8–9 says, "For by grace you have been saved through faith; and that not of yourselves, it is the gift of God; not as a result of works, so that no one may boast." You were saved by grace through faith and that is the same way you will live a life of freedom. Believe that God will do what you cannot see. It is He who brings about freedom. Freedom comes by grace through faith.

In order to access God's grace, you must acknowledge your need for it. What is your need? Do you need grace because of sin? Do you need grace for spiritual growth? Do you need grace to tell your story? What are the areas in your life in which you need grace? Don't struggle to be better. Don't vow to try harder. Acknowledge *your need* of His all-sufficient grace, and move forward in His power.

You were saved by faith; therefore, live by faith. We can't, but God can. Perhaps you don't have self-control of your eating habits. God can help you. Perhaps you can't tell others your story, but God can help you. God enables you.

After you acknowledge your need for His grace, simply believe Him. Why is it so difficult to believe in and rely on God's grace? Because we have to believe in something we cannot see. Faith releases God's grace. Faith is the key that unlocks the door to the unmerited favor of God. God's grace releases power to live the Christian life. Grace is never based on who you are apart from Him or on what you can do. Grace is always based on who He is and what He has done. That's why the story of your past is so powerful. It paints a picture of who God is and what He has done in your life.

Rescued to Help Rescue

God is our Redeemer. A redeemer is someone who rescues and delivers. When we are in slavery or bondage, what we need first is a redeemer. Once God has redeemed us, He wants to work through us to redeem others, too.

The story of Moses in the Bible shows that God uses imperfect persons to show His redemptive power to others. You may already know the story well; you can find it in the Bible book of Exodus. When God's people were enslaved in Egypt, God used Moses to bring them out of captivity and take them to the promised land He had set aside for them. God used someone who had a past: Moses had fled Egypt after killing a man. God used someone who felt inadequate: Moses had a speech impediment. God used someone who seemed to others to be useless: Moses was just a sheepherder. But through Moses, God showed the people that He was their Redeemer, their rescuer.

God wants to rescue you, too; He wants to rescue you out of your captivity to lies. After He rescues you, He wants to use you to help rescue others.

You can't free yourself. God has to rescue you, because you are enslaved to sin. Having a poor body image isn't just an unhealthy habit—it's a sin. When you do not treat your God-made body with respect, it's a sin. We need to get to a point where we realize this truth. We cannot experience freedom until we realize that we need to be free. We need to have a change in our thinking. We need to turn in a new direction.

Change Direction—Repent

I don't have the greatest sense of direction. When I am driving my car north, I feel like I am driving south. Therefore, I make many wrong turns. I have to rely heavily on printed directions. One day, I decided to go visit a friend who lived in Manhattan Beach near Los Angeles. I lived about 45 minutes south in Orange County. I had no clue where I was going, so I printed out directions from an Internet site. I had trusted that site before, and its directions had taken me to my destination. This time I had the same faith that the printed directions would lead me to my friend's front door.

As I was driving on the freeway, I saw a sign for the exit I was supposed to take. I looked at the directions again for confirmation. The directions advised me to turn right off the exit ramp. I knew that when traveling north in California, the beach is always on the left, but since I had experienced success using directions from this site before, against my better judgment, I turned right. I drove a little ways and began to notice that things looked strange. I noticed bars on the windows. I noticed suspicious-looking people standing in circles. I quickly realized I was in a dangerous neighborhood, so I made a U-turn at the next intersection. I had believed wrong information and had gone the wrong way.

> *The truth about repentance is that it leads to salvation.*

I tell you this story not to confess my poor driving abilities, but to show you the spiritual parallel. When we sin by abusing the body God gave us, it's as if we have made a wrong turn. We need to make a U-turn and begin to see our bodies the way God sees them. Turning totally in the other direction is called repentance. We need to turn from our sin with regard to our faulty body image.

Repentance is certainly not the most popular subject. I think most people are scared to talk about repentance because the word itself causes people to feel uncomfortable. This is a message that God has been teaching me for the past few months. True repentance requires us to be stripped of our pride, admit that we are wrong, and be willing to submit ourselves to the mercy and grace of God.

Repentance is a matter of the heart. God wants our heart. He wants truth in our innermost being. When you experience repentance, you gain a changed perspective. You begin to see sin the way God sees sin. You begin to see yourself the way God sees you.

The truth about repentance is that it leads us to salvation. Some of you reading this book might never have experienced the freedom brought about by salvation. If you have never trusted Christ as your Savior, I urge you to start your journey towards freedom right now by trusting in Jesus—the most trustworthy person you will ever know. Don't be ashamed to admit you need Him—we all have the need to repent. Paul expressed our fallen state in his letter to the Romans: *"For all have sinned and fall short of the glory of God"* (Romans 3:23). Pray right now, asking Jesus to take control of your life, and then find a fellowship of Christians to support you and walk with you.

If you are a believer, repentance leads to restoration for you. We often hear that someone rededicated his life to the Lord. In college, I majored in public relations; in that field, the word rededication means "to take a bad situation and twist it to look good." That happens all the time in the media. But rededication in the spiritual sense is a word that means "repentance." Repentance causes us to acknowledge our sin. It causes us to come to our senses. Unfortunately, most of the time, we have to reach a miserable state before we will do this.

The Gifts of Repentance

Look at what repentance brings us according to God's Word:

> *Therefore repent and return, so that your sins may be wiped away, in order that times of refreshing may come from the presence of the Lord.*
> —Acts 3:19

Repentance brings about a time of **refreshing**. David asked God to restore unto him the joy of God's great salvation (Psalm 51:12), and David testified of what that restoration is like:

> *How blessed is he whose transgression is forgiven,*
> *Whose sin is covered!*
> *How blessed is the man to whom the LORD does not*
>   *impute iniquity,*
> *And in whose spirit there is no deceit!*
> —Psalm 32:1–2

When we truly repent of our sin with regard to our bodies, we will see **restoration**. *"How blessed"* we will be! God will restore our mind to truth. God's mercies are new every morning, and He will give us a fresh beginning daily.

When we repent, it leads us to **worship**. I have dedicated a whole chapter to learning to worship God with your body, but it is important to see that it is repentance that leads you to worship. Only after we have repented and experienced salvation or repented and experienced restoration can we experience true worship.

> *Who may ascend into the hill of the LORD?*
> *And who may stand in His holy place?*
> *He who has clean hands and a pure heart,*
> *Who has not lifted up his soul to falsehood*
> *And has not sworn deceitfully.*
> —Psalm 24:3–4

Repentance gives us clean hands and a pure heart. Repentance, you could say, is the highway into the presence of God.

It is not until we truly repent that we are able to experience those times of refreshing that come from the presence of the Lord. A person who has experienced true repentance knows the graciousness and mercy of God. When you have tasted the kindness of God, you will want to share it with others. You will want to help point others to that kindness.

You and I were created to represent God to others. As Christians, our life is all about God and His glory. Let's remember that: It's not all about us—it's all about Him. I have discovered that when I step back and recognize it's not about me, but it's all about Him, that is the time when God uses me the most. No matter what my story entails, God wants to use me.

Live Intentionally

My husband played soccer for about six years when he was a child. In the last game of his last season of playing, he played defense. The game was tied, and the other team brought the ball down the field. Scott ran up to kick the ball away from his goal, but completely missed the ball! As his foot came back down, he kicked the ball right into his own goal. In life, we often times kick the ball into our own goal. We work against ourselves.

We end up playing for the other team. Every time we believe lies and fall back into deception, we kick the ball into the wrong goal. In order to kick the ball into the right goal, we need to live intentionally.

We tend to live for ourselves. We tend to think about what makes us feel good. We tend to think about what we want to do. But the purpose of our life is far greater than our own personal fulfillment, our peace of mind, or even our happiness. It is far greater than our family, our career, or even our dreams and ambitions. We were born by His purpose and for His purpose. Colossians 1:16 says, *"For by Him all things were created, both in the heavens and on earth, visible and invisible, whether thrones or dominions or rulers or authorities—all things have been created through Him and for Him."* You were created with a purpose. God wants you to live an intentional life. Intentional means "to be done on purpose; deliberate." That is the kind of life God is calling us to lead. He wants us to live intentionally. We can either live for ourselves or choose to live an intentional life for God. We can live in defeat because we struggled through an ugly, prideful disorder, or we can allow God to use it for His glory.

One Intentional Plan of God

One story of the Bible is especially entrancing to those of us who love to watch beauty pageants. It's a true story of God using a young woman to bring about His purposes. Esther was a beautiful Jewish girl who was chosen to be part of the King of Persia's harem. She received every luxurious beauty treatment available for six months (sounds great!), and when the king held sort of a beauty pageant to help him choose a wife from his harem, he chose Esther.

But the king did not realize that Esther was a Jew. Her cousin Mordecai, who raised Esther after she was orphaned, was one of a group of Jews brought to Persia as captives. When Mordecai learned of a plot to kill all the Jews in Persia, he begged Esther to use her influence with the king to prevent the massacre.

Esther hesitated. It had been 30 days since the king had asked to see her. If anyone entered the king's presence without being summoned, they were to be killed unless the king held out his scepter to show he wanted to spare them. She would be risking her life. When Mordecai heard of Esther's hesitation, he sent her this message:

*Do not think that because you are in the king's house you alone of all the Jews will escape. For if you remain silent at this time, relief and deliverance for the Jews will arise from another place, but you and your father's family will perish. **And who knows but that you have come to royal position for such a time as this?***

—Esther 4:13–14 (NIV; bold added for emphasis)

Mordecai was suggesting God had placed her in this royal position for a purpose: *"for such a time as this."* She was there to intercede for her people. Esther did take the risk of going into the king's presence. To find out what happened, read the rest of the book of Esther in the Bible. It's a great story!

When God redeems and restores you, He also gives you a purpose. God has many divine purposes to accomplish in this world. God wants to use you to accomplish His purposes. Esther was in a unique position of power because of her life experiences. When God heals you of your body image problems, you then are in a unique position to help others who suffer. God wants to use your past for His purposes.

How do you live an intentional life? You begin to live for God's purposes—for God's glory. Romans 11:36 reminds us that, *"For from Him and through Him and to Him are all things. To Him be the glory forever. Amen."* In all you do, think about His glory. When you look at yourself in the mirror, think of His glory. When you decide what to eat, think of His glory.

*Whether, then, you eat or drink or whatever you do, **do all to the glory of God.***

—1 Corinthians 10:31 (bold added for emphasis)

Intentionally Invest in Relationships

To live an intentional life, begin to live for relationships. The best way to allow God to use your past is to invest in relationships.

Invest in people who will help you grow in your faith and in truth. Intentionally seek out people who can help you grow. God places these people in our lives. They have more experience and more wisdom than we do. My mentor has invested so much of herself in me. She is the one who pushed me towards freedom. She is the one who spoke truth into my life. She is the one who made me look beyond myself to see the damage to my future children that my path of lies might cause. As I intentionally allowed someone to help me grow, I began to allow God to use my past.

Not only do you need to invest time in people who help you grow, but you also need to **invest in people who need your help to grow.** Intentionally look for people into whom you can pour your life. I feel useless if I do not pass on to others what God has taught me. Passing on helpful insights and information to others to help them avoid or overcome problems similar to the ones I experienced makes my past suffering worthwhile. Allow God to use your past to help heal someone else.

This last relationship to be mentioned is of *primary* importance: intentionally **invest in a relationship with God.** Intentionally experience life with Him. Intentionally spend time with Him. Intentionally talk to Him. Real life comes through knowing God and seeking after Him.

A. W. Tozer, in his book *The Pursuit of God*, said, "Come near to the holy men and women of the past and you will soon feel the heat of their desire after God. They mourned for Him, they prayed and wrestled and sought for Him day and night, in season and out, and when they had found Him the finding was all the sweeter for the long seeking."

Be willing to let go of your past, and allow God to use you and it. Know that He will fulfill His promise of freedom and purpose in you. You have a choice to make. Are you going to just play the game with no purpose, or are you going to live an intentional life for God? God has a purpose for your life. God put you here *"for such a time as this."*

Bible Study Questions

1 Memorize Esther 4:14. Write it down on a card and carry it with you this week.

2 Do you need to repent or make a U-turn because of the way you have treated your body?

3 Write a prayer to God asking for forgiveness for the way you have treated or thought about your body. Allow Him to restore you and comfort you.

4 Read 2 Corinthians 1:3–7. Why does God comfort us?

5 Why would God want to use your past?

6 How do you think God can begin to use your past?

7 Can you think of anyone into whom you can intentionally pour your life?

Body. Beauty. Boys.

Write your reactions to Sarah's thoughts in this chapter. Which thoughts relate to you? Which ones don't relate to you? How did you feel as you read?

_____

_____

_____

_____

_____

_____

_____

_____

_____

_____

_____

_____

_____

_____

_____

_____

_____

CHAPTER EIGHT

What Is Your Focus?

We have come to the end of our journey together. During this journey, maybe you have realized that you have believed lies about your body. Maybe you have learned that Jesus is the way to freedom. But you may still wonder, "What now? How do I stay free every day?" For some people, freedom is scary because bondage is all they've ever known. I fought a battle for freedom from my body image problem for more than a decade. When I began to taste freedom, it was foreign to me. I didn't know what it was like to wake up and not be consumed with thoughts about my body, what I was going to eat, and how much I was going to exercise that day.

Stepping into freedom can be scary because it requires faith. It would be easier to believe if you could see God or touch Him, but faith is trusting even when we can't see. Second Corinthians 3:17 says, *"Now the Lord is the Spirit, and where the Spirit of the Lord is, there is liberty."* When Christ brought salvation, He brought freedom. Salvation brings freedom *from* sin and freedom *over* sin. Freedom comes in knowing God and respecting Him. When you learn to respect God, you learn how to respect the body He gave you.

The solution to our daily struggle is to fix our eyes on Jesus. Sometimes I would get so caught up in what it would take to not struggle that it would overwhelm me. God is asking us to not worry about tomorrow, not to focus on our circumstances, but to focus our eyes on Him…today.

Discarding Old Habits

As we begin to focus on God, we will notice some of our old habits will have to bite the dust.

Anxiety must go. Jesus tells us to not be anxious about tomorrow and what we will eat or what we will wear:

"Do not worry then, saying, 'What will we eat?' or 'What will we drink?' or 'What will we wear for clothing?' For the Gentiles eagerly seek all these things; for your heavenly Father knows that you need all these things. But seek first His kingdom and His righteousness, and all these things will be added to you. So do not worry about tomorrow; for tomorrow will care for itself. Each day has enough trouble of its own."
—Matthew 6:31–34

Encumbrances must be laid aside. In Hebrews, Paul describes life as a race. We are to lay aside the things that entangle us.

Therefore, since we have so great a cloud of witnesses surrounding us, let us also lay aside every encumbrance and the sin which so easily entangles us, and let us run with endurance the race that is set before us, fixing our eyes on Jesus, the author and perfecter of faith, who for the joy set before Him endured the cross, despising the shame, and has sat down at the right hand of the throne of God. For consider Him who has endured such hostility by sinners against Himself, so that you will not grow weary and lose heart.
—Hebrews 12:1–3

In college I used to play tennis. I had to run to train. I hated running in the winter because it would be so cold outside that I would need to wear a sweatshirt—and I hated wearing a sweatshirt because sweatshirts are bulky and they make it more difficult to run. Sweatshirts are an encumbrance to me when running.

One of my high school friends who was an outstanding athlete began competing in triathlons when he entered college. When he ran, he literally threw to the side everything that would hinder his performance. He prepared himself to run. He wore no shirt and very little in the way of shorts. He even shaved his legs! He ran freely because nothing, no sweatshirt or anything else, entangled him.

We, too, need to lay aside the things that entangle us. What would that be for you? Think about what keeps you from *running freely*. I had to stop reading certain magazines to disentangle myself from my poor body image cycle. The pictures in the magazines constantly pushed me to compare myself. I had to stop watching celebrity gossip television shows. I was obsessed with them, but those shows only entangled me. I couldn't run freely when I was tangled up in those thoughts.

What is it that keeps you from running freely? **Lay it aside.**

Choosing Your Focus

Let's really be honest with each other. What do you focus on most? Do you focus on the mirror or on what God says to be true about you? There will be a lifelong need to continuously refocus on God's truth. To be honest with you, I still have days in which I focus on the mirror rather than the truth that was spoken by my Creator.

How do you focus on God? How do you *not* focus on the mirror? God wants us to enjoy Him rather than focusing on our body's imperfections. Let me try to shed some light on what a life of freedom looks like. I want to show you what happens when you focus your eyes on Christ and throw off all that entangles you. Look at what Psalm 37 says:

> *Do not fret because of evildoers,*
> *Be not envious toward wrongdoers.*
> *For they will wither quickly like the grass*
> *And fade like the green herb.*
> *Trust in the LORD and do good;*
> *Dwell in the land and cultivate faithfulness.*
> **Delight yourself in the LORD;**
> **And He will give you the desires of your heart.**
> *Commit your way to the LORD,*
> *Trust also in Him, and He will do it.*
> *He will bring forth your righteousness as the light*
> *And your judgment as the noonday.*
> *Rest in the LORD and wait patiently for Him;*
> *Do not fret because of him who prospers in his way,*
> *Because of the man who carries out wicked schemes.*
> —Psalm 37:1–7 (bold added for emphasis)

I want to show you how to have a relationship with God in which you delight in Him and He delights in you. Delight isn't a word that you hear much these days. It may even seem kind of old fashioned, but something about the concept of delight has always intrigued me. Delight, to me, means an exciting love. Delight is simply enjoying something extremely. Delight is creating snow angels or rolling down a hill or doing a cartwheel. Delight is love having fun.

That's the kind of relationship God wants to have with you—the kind of relationship that does not focus on the mirror, but on the Creator. Do you have fun with God? Have you ever even thought about your relationship with God being fun? Does being His child excite you? Do you notice the little things He does for you? Do you notice the big things He does for you? When you begin to focus your eyes on Him, you begin to see Him in *everything*.

My husband and I were traveling back from a visit to my parents' home, and we had to stop at our church on the way to our home because he had a meeting. While he was in the meeting, I decided to take a walk.

Normally when I go for a walk, I have my iPod pumping music in my ears to help the time pass, but I did not have my iPod that day. Since

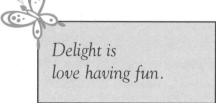

Delight is love having fun.

I was walking around an empty parking lot, I decided talk out loud to God as I walked. Sometimes when we exercise, we focus on how many calories we can burn. But that day as I walked, God spoke to my heart about the need to focus my eyes on Him. I saw a beautiful sunset, and it was as if He wrote His desire for my attention all over the sky. If I had been focused on counting calories rather than focusing on God, I might have missed Him delighting me.

I love caramel mochas from Starbucks. But I have to be honest with you: Sometimes they just don't make them right. Sometimes a bad shot of espresso ruins the whole experience. I now ask God to enable the person making the caramel mocha, the flavor that thrills my taste buds, to do it right. I know it might sound crazy to you, but I believe that God knows what delights me, and He would love to let me enjoy Him through a caramel mocha.

I love everything about the sky. I love the clouds, the stars, and the sun. Sometimes I am completely taken aback by the absolute beauty of a sunset. God paints it for me! He knows that sunsets thrill me, and I will praise Him for what He has done when I see one. God wants you to focus your eyes on Him. The more you focus on Him, the more He shows you Himself in everything around you.

My mom loves cats. She always has—ever since she was a little girl. She gets so excited when she finds a new cat. From time to time, she prays that God will bring her a cat. In fact, that's how most of our cats have arrived at our house in the past. One night during the summer, we were just enjoying being outside when we saw something moving in the yard. We crept toward where we saw the movement, and to our surprise, we found two tiny kittens! They were the cutest things ever. The next day, my mom found a third one. I told her that God was just delighting her. He knew that she would be thrilled to have one kitten, but God gave her three. That is just like our God! He wants you to enjoy Him.

The more you focus your eyes on God, the less you focus on your-self. When we focus on ourselves, disappointment inevitably follows. Disappointment comes when expectations aren't met. We are left wanting.

For me, disappointment used to happen every year on Valentine's Day. The day is an annual setup for disappointment. I dreaded it every year when I was in high school. Throughout the day, people would arrive to drop off flower arrangements, balloons, and candy to be delivered to the students. At the end of each period, a list of names would be called out. If your name was called, that usually meant someone had dropped off a present for you, and you could go pick it up. Every year, I waited for my name to be called. Year after year, it didn't happen. I was always disap-pointed. That particular disappointment occurred because I was focused on what I was going to get from someone. To find freedom, you can't focus on what others can give you, but on what God can give you. If you look for others to make you feel good about yourself, you will be disappointed. But when you begin to find your fulfillment in Christ alone, you will find a life of delight.

Sometimes it works the opposite way. We focus not on what we receive, but on what we can give to others, and we are left wanting. At the root of our intent, we might realize that we give in order to find appreciation and approval. We focus on making someone else think that we are priceless and significant. Do you realize that *Someone* already does think you're priceless? The same Someone who created you is the One who spoke and the stars popped into their places. He's the same One who causes the sun to rise.

Sometimes focusing on our hopes sets us up for disappointment. Proverbs 13:12 says, *"Hope deferred makes the heart sick."* We set our hope on a lot of things. On what do you set your hope? Whatever it is, it will likely bring disappointment until you find freedom and contentment by focusing your eyes on the Author and Perfecter of your faith.

Developing Your Relationship with God

What does it look like to have this kind of relationship with God? Most all women desire, whether secretly or not so secretly, to have a relationship with a man. Let me tell you what a relationship with a man looks like and how it is similar to a relationship with God.

Get to know each other. You cannot have a relationship with someone until you get to know that person. The same is true with God. You have to get to know the One on whom you are to focus. You get to know Him by experiencing Him. How do you experience Him? You communicate with Him. You talk to Him.

When I first began dating Scott, who is now my husband, we would talk for hours on the phone. Even if we had gone out on a date that night, we would still talk for hours on the phone after our date. I've never been a phone talker, but I became one with him because I had met someone special. I just couldn't get enough of him. With him, I could talk for hours about anything! I would look at the clock and wonder where the time went! It's because I *wanted* to know him. I wanted to know *everything* about him.

The same is somewhat true with God. He wants you to get to know Him. He can't get enough of you. Your relationship with God is more wonderful than any earthly relationship. In close relationships, there comes a point at which you know practically everything about someone; it's not quite that way with God. The more we know about Him, the more we realize we don't know, and the more we want to know even more! Getting to know God is a progressive work with no end but enormous rewards. Paul describes to the Philippians his longing to know God better:

[For my determined purpose is] that I may know Him [that I may progressively become more deeply and intimately acquainted with Him, perceiving and recognizing and understanding the wonders of His Person more strongly and more clearly], and that I may in that same way come to know the power outflowing from His resurrection.
—Philippians 3:10 (AMP)

Do you know the wonders of His person? Have you even begun to know Him? He is majesty; His is the glory; He is the best part of all existence.

Hang out together. When you are in a relationship with someone, you hang out together. You go on dates. You spend time together. Do you do that with God? He wants you to hang out with Him. Set aside some time every day to hang out with God. God has written you the greatest love letter you will ever read. The Bible is His love letter to you. Spending time in the Bible is one way to hang out with God.

After I had been dating Scott for a month or so, I had a speaking engagement on a tiny island in the South Pacific. This island was a six-hour flight from Hawaii. There was about a 12-hour time difference between that island and where Scott was, so we did not talk much by phone. We did, however, communicate daily through email. Every day, I would sit down at the computer and wait anxiously for his email to appear. I would read it over and over and over. I soaked up every word. If someone had asked me what he said, I could have repeated it word for word. Do you read God's love letter—His Word—like that? Do you soak up every word? If someone asked what He said, could you repeat it word for word?

Receive the gifts offered. One of the joys of having a relationship here on earth is receiving gifts. I love to receive gifts because it means someone thought specifically about me. Scott and I had been dating for about two months when I walked into my office one morning and found a pink rose on my desk with a note that spoke of his affinity for me and excitement about our relationship. God wants to give you gifts. God wants to make you smile. When you focus your eyes on Him, you begin to behold Him in everything and begin to take note of all the blessings—both big and little—that He sends your way.

∫hare affection. Finally, God has affection for you, and when you have a relationship with Him, you can experience that affection. He wants to satisfy your craving for affection in a way that surpasses human touch. Isaiah 54:5 says, *"For your husband is your Maker, whose name is the LORD of hosts; and your Redeemer is the Holy One of Israel, who is called the God of all the earth."* As your Redeemer, God wants to fulfill the duties of a relationship. He wants you to be satisfied and not feel the need to look for affection elsewhere. God wants you to delight in Him, and He wants to delight you.

For me, one of the most amazing moments with the Lord happened about a month ago. I was working at a women's conference in Mobile, Alabama. One of my spiritual mentors was speaking, and at the end of the weekend, she closed with something very cool. She began to explain how she had just renewed her marriage vows with her husband on their 25th anniversary. She went on to repeat the vows that she had made with him. I was standing and listening in the back hallway—all alone. I pictured a wedding in my head. I could imagine walking toward Jesus. I could imagine standing face to face. In that moment, with tear-filled eyes, I began to quietly say those same vows to my Husband, my Maker. I took vows to delight in my Lord forever. God will delight you more than any human man ever could. He wants you to focus your eyes on a relationship with Him and accept His affection.

Getting Focused on God

What would you do if you found out that you had a terminal disease? How would your life change if you knew your days were limited? Would that fact draw your life into focus? Your answer depends on your faith. If you have no faith, it might not matter what you do from now on. But if you have faith, you realize that there is more to life than just getting through the day. You would live as if your life mattered. You would live with a real sense of purpose.

Do you now live like you have a purpose? Do you know what your chief end is? The Westminster Shorter Catechism says, "Man's chief end is to glorify God, and to enjoy Him forever."

Worship God. If man's chief end is to glorify God, tell me, do you? Do you worship God or just give Him lip service? Do you focus on Him or is your focus more on the mirror?

Whether you are a Christian or not, we all worship something. Worship is simply giving something or someone worth. Do you give worth to God and His Word or to what you see in the mirror? So many times I look in the mirror and give it more worth than what God's Word says is true. We have already talked about how to worship God with our bodies, but I think it is important to address worship as it relates to our daily focus. Whatever we focus on is what we worship.

One aspect of worship is giving something or someone your time. When you focus on your body, you are giving it time. So much of my time used to be devoted to exercise and to thinking through what I was eating. When I did that, I worshiped my body. I was not focusing my eyes on God.

Worship is valuable to God because it takes you time to do it. You give that time to God, and are blessed by doing so. When you are enthralled with your body, it also takes time, but what lasting return do you get from time spent that way? Your time is stolen from you. How much time do you waste in thinking about food and exercise? God is asking for your time. He is asking for wholehearted devotion. He is asking for your focused attention.

I have been struck by my lack of thinking about daily worship. I think about worship on Sundays. I think about worship off and on, but I usually do not think of worshiping in everything I do. My worship and adoration of Him is sometimes sporadic and, honestly, sometimes a bit shallow. It seems like often it is about me rather than about Him.

God wants us to worship Him with all our heart and mind. When we do, He takes notice and reveals more of Himself to us. David spoke of this to his son Solomon.

> *"As for you, my son Solomon, know the God of your father, and serve Him with a whole heart and a willing mind; for the LORD searches all hearts, and understands every intent of the thoughts. If you seek Him, He will let you find Him; but if you forsake Him, He will reject you forever."*
> —1 Chronicles 28:9

God wants you to focus on Him with your *whole* heart. Second Chronicles 25:2 says of King Amaziah that he *"did right in the sight of the LORD, yet not with a whole heart."* He had a heart problem. Why did he serve God halfheartedly? He focused his eyes on seeking revenge for his father's death. This was contrary to God's Word. When we focus on our mirror, we are acting contrary to God's Word. That's when we begin to love God only halfheartedly. You can't allow part of you to focus what the world thinks. You must totally focus on what God says to be true. How would you feel if a man proposed to you, saying, "I will love you with all my heart for 364 days of the year, but one day a year, I will be with other women"? Would you accept his proposal? No way! You wouldn't want halfhearted commitment; you would want *wholehearted devotion*.

> *Time is fleeting. Life is flying by. In what have you invested your time?*

Live with purpose. Psalm 90:12 speaks of the need to live with purpose: "*So teach us to number our days, that we may present to You a heart of wisdom.*" This psalm is a lament of Moses mourning over the wasted years of Israel. At this point, Israel had been wandering in the wilderness for almost 40 years. The people had a lack of purpose and significance. If you were to die tomorrow, what would someone say of your life? For what would they remember you? Would they remember that you focused on God or on the mirror? Moses gives us some wise advice in this psalm. He says to number the days of our lives. Be aware that the commodity of time is limited. Time is fleeting. Life is flying by. In what have you invested your time?

We must spend our time on something that matters. If we are worshiping something that matters, our bodies don't matter that much. At the end of your life, what will you have done? Will you have lived life with a purpose? Will you have lived life focused on the Author and Perfecter of your faith?

I had a friend who died unexpectedly. My friend was not a believer. I went to her funeral, and as I sat and listened to her eulogy, I cried. The priest talked about what she had focused on, and it had nothing to do with God. She had missed the point of life. So many days had been wasted. If you were at the end of your journey, what would you say when God asked what you had done with your life? On what would you have spent your time? God deserves your focus.

Build character. We need to look at life the way the author of Hebrews did: as a race. We must train and prepare effectively for it. Learning to focus on God during this life takes effort and training. Having a good relationship with God takes practice. Developing the character God wants in us is hard work.

When I was in college, I was on the tennis team, so I had to work out a lot, whether I wanted to or not. Our practice every afternoon included lots of running and conditioning. In the winter, we would meet at 6:00 A.M. to run and lift weights. Conditioning was one of those things that I both loved and hated. I loved the way it got me into shape for the season, but I hated how much sacrifice and physical pain it took.

My coach developed a weight plan to help me build muscle. I wanted to build up my muscle so that I would be a better athlete. The thing about building muscle is that it takes a lot of time. Sometimes it hurts, sometimes it is frustrating, but it's always rewarding. Most people give up after a week in the gym because it's too hard.

The same is true with our character. God is in the process of building our character. He wants us to have a character that reflects Him. The truth is that it is a challenge to pursue that type of character. Just like building muscle, building character takes discipline and perseverance. We would rather spend time working on our outward appearance than take the time to build character. That is contrary to God's perspective as stated in 1 Samuel 16:7: *"for God sees not as man sees, for man looks at the outward appearance, but the LORD looks at the heart."* What kind of heart is God looking for? The psalmist knew that God was looking for a pure heart when he wrote the following words:

> *Who may ascend into the hill of the LORD?*
> *And who may stand in His holy place?*
> **He who has clean hands and a pure heart,**
> *Who has not lifted up his soul to falsehood*
> *And has not sworn deceitfully.*
> *He shall receive a blessing from the LORD*
> *And righteousness from the God of his salvation.*
> —Psalm 24:3–5 (bold added for emphasis)

In order to build muscle, you have to practice. The same is true spiritually. In order to build character you have to practice. If you want to be a woman who does not focus on the mirror, but focuses on God, then you need to practice the kind of character traits God is looking for, namely a *pure heart*. God desires purity in the way we think about ourselves. To be pure means to be chosen, clear, sincere, and empty of self. What would it look like to be pure in our thoughts, heart, and our actions? How can you be sincere and empty of self in your thoughts, motives, and actions?

We need to purify ourselves through sacrifice and obedience. When you take the focus off yourself and put it on God, you make a sacrifice. It wouldn't be a sacrifice if we didn't like or want what we were giving up to God. I want to focus on my body. I want to be the best looking person around, but God wants me to focus on Him. In John 3:30, John the Baptist said of Jesus, *"He must become greater; I must become less"* (NIV). God's Word promises to prosper those who obey Him. He wants you to obey Him and focus your eyes on Him. This kind of character requires sacrifice and obedience.

Move from anxiety to peace. Women have a tendency to be anxious about many things, including their appearance. Paul's advice is to not be anxious about anything, but rather pray to God about issues that concern us:

> *Be anxious for nothing, but in everything by prayer and supplication with thanksgiving let your requests be made known to God. And the peace of God, which surpasses all comprehension, will guard your hearts and your minds in Christ Jesus.*
> —Philippians 4:6–7

As we pray, offer thanks, and make our requests, then the peace of God guards our hearts and minds. Peace is the absence or end of strife. The opposite of peace is strife. On days when I struggle with my body, I live in strife. There is no peace. On those days especially, I need to do as Paul suggests: pray, petition God, and give thanks! Just refocus on God—that's the way to move from anxiety to peace.

Set your mind on things of God. Another way to focus your eyes on God is set your minds on the things of God.

> *Therefore if you have been raised up with Christ, keep seeking the things above, where Christ is, seated at the right hand*

of God. Set your mind on the things above, not on the things
that are on earth.
—Colossians 3:1–2

What does that look like? How do we do that?

> *Finally, brethren, whatever is true, whatever is honorable,*
> *whatever is right, whatever is pure, whatever is lovely, what-*
> *ever is of good repute, if there is any excellence and if anything*
> *worthy of praise, dwell on these things.*
> —Philippians 4:8

To dwell on something is to think about or meditate on something. To dwell means to take up residency. We need to begin to take up residency in truth. You must program your mind to think or dwell on things above. It is not natural to do this. You must *choose* to do this. It is an act of will.

Think about it. Decision making is not a problem for animals, but it is for us human because we have a will. The will enables us to obey in spite of our feelings. Most the time, we cannot control our emotions, but we can control our will. Whatever enters our mind, we need to put it up against God's truth. If it doesn't glorify God, then we need to turn our minds to things that do.

Every night before I go to bed, I go to the kitchen and prepare the coffeemaker to do its thing the next morning (I have one of those coffeemakers with an automatic timer). Every night by habit, I set the timer for 15 minutes before I plan to wake up. In the morning when my alarm goes off, the only thing that gets me up out of the bed is knowing the coffee is already made and awaiting me. I picture the same thing with our minds. Setting our minds on things above needs to become a habit. We need to program truth into our minds so that when the morning comes, we are ready to live in freedom.

Paul makes a powerful statement in verse 13 of Philippians 4: *"I can do all things through Him who strengthens me."* You can live a life of freedom through Him who strengthens you. Every day, God will enable you to dwell on things above. It is His strength, not your own, that will enable you to find contentment in yourself.

I pray that you are not like the women that Paul described in his letter to Timothy:

> *For among them are those who enter into households and captivate weak women weighed down with sins, led on by various impulses, always learning and never able to come to the knowledge of the truth.*
> —2 Timothy 3:6–7

Paul described these women as weak because they were weighed down by sin and led on by various impulses. When you struggle with body image issues, you are mostly living from impulse to impulse.

The worst thing about these women was that fact that they were always learning, but never able to understand the truth. How terrible! It would be a shame to devote time to learning the truth about what God says about you, but never to live it out in your life. The Greek word for truth is *aletheia*, which is the "unveiled reality of an appearance." *Aletheia* denotes the reality lying clearly in front of you. May God's truth denote what is clearly in front of you. Circumstances will come your way that will tempt you to focus on your body and not on God. Get in God's Word daily and allow it to cleanse your mind. Refocus on God's truth every day and live it out.

Bible Study Questions

1 Memorize Philippians 4:8. Write it on a card and carry it with you this week.

2 Read 1 Chronicles 28:9. According to this verse, what are you supposed to do?

3 Do you enjoy your relationship with God?

4 Is anything missing from your relationship with God? If so, what can you do about it?

5 Read Hebrews 12:1–2. How can you throw off that which hinders you?

6 Do you focus on God or on what you see in the mirror?

7 Write a prayer to God telling Him your desire to dwell on the things above, and ask His help in doing so.

Body. Beauty. Boys.

Write your reactions to Sarah's thoughts in this chapter. Which thoughts relate to you? Which ones don't relate to you? How did you feel as you read?

_____

_____

_____

_____

_____

_____

_____

_____

_____

_____

_____

_____

_____

_____

_____

_____

_____

_____

Conclusion

Anyone who knows both my mother and me sees an amazing resemblance between us. In my parents' house, there is a portrait of my mother on her wedding day. I can't tell you how many people have walked into our house and asked whether I had been married long ago, thinking it was me in the portrait. Not only do I bear a striking physical resemblance to my mother, but I also do many things just like she does. While growing up, I watched my mother sit in a comfy chair with a cup of coffee and study her Bible every morning. She had me memorizing Scripture before I could even read. She would write the verse out on a note card and then draw pictures to illustrate the words. She taught me how to study the Bible inductively when I was only in elementary school. She taught me the power of prayer when I was only a toddler. I am who I am today partly because my mother poured herself into me.

Leaving a Legacy

My mom has left her legacy in me. I have a legacy to leave with you. You have a legacy to leave with others. You have a captive audience around you. Someone is always watching. We all—whether married with no children, married with children, single again, or never-married single—have someone to whom we may leave a legacy. You do not have to have children in order to leave a legacy.

> *"For I will pour out water on the thirsty land*
> *And streams on the dry ground;*

I will pour out My Spirit on your offspring
And My blessing on your descendants;
And they will spring up among the grass
Like poplars by streams of water.
This one will say, 'I am the LORD'S';
And that one will call on the name of Jacob;
And another will write on his hand, 'Belonging to the LORD,'
And will name Israel's name with honor."
—Isaiah 44:3–5

These passages are talking about Israel. If you are a Christian, you are a spiritual descendant of Abraham. Galatians 3:29 says, *"And if you belong to Christ, then you are Abraham's descendants, heirs according to promise."* We have offspring who need to be left a legacy of the Lord. Most all books on leadership would teach that in leadership, success is succession. If those coming behind me are not able to take what I have offered and incorporate it into their lives and build on it, then I have failed as a leader. I believe the same is true spiritually. You are successful if your offspring succeed you. I want to leave a legacy in you not because I want to succeed, but because I want you to succeed me. I have experienced a life of freedom, and I desire for you to experience life beyond that.

To leave a legacy that goes beyond accomplishment alone, a woman must devote herself to matters of the heart. We must develop character. We are set up to fail if we never think about our heart and what kind of person we should be. We could try all day long to fix the person on the outside, but we will fail if we never address issues of the heart.

Character is what makes someone worth following. A worldview is the way you see things. Young women, what kind of character are you displaying to younger women? Do you display a heart that cares only about the outward appearance? Do you display a heart that knows real freedom in Christ? When your life is over, for what do you want to be remembered? What legacy should you leave or want to leave?

To help answer that question, think about what you want to become. What you do will flow from who you are. What appears on the outside will only reflect what is on the inside. I created a standard of the kind of woman I want to be. I want to be refined, discerning, wise, sensible, pure, and sensitive; I want to be a woman who thirsts for righteousness, digs into God's Word, and knows the truth. These words form a boundary around my actions. If I want to be this kind of woman, then I need to begin taking steps toward this. I need to develop these characteristics in my heart. To leave a legacy that is not merely superficial, you must devote yourself to matters of the heart.

I want to leave a legacy of truth and freedom, but how do I do that? How do we leave such a legacy? It is simple enough—just pass it on:

> *"So now I charge you in the sight of all Israel and of the assembly of the LORD, and in the hearing of our God: Be careful to follow all the commands of the LORD your God, that you may possess this good land and pass it on as an inheritance to your descendants forever."*
> —1 Chronicles 28:8 (NIV)

Pass it on. However, you cannot pass on anything that you do not possess. I cannot pass on one million dollars if I do not have a million dollars. I cannot pass on freedom if I am not free myself. I cannot pass on contentment if I am not content myself. The answer is that you become what you want others to be. I become free so that I can lead you to become free. I become content so that I can lead you to become content.

Fail, But Get Back Up

In order to leave a legacy of truth, we need to learn to walk in truth. We learned in an earlier chapter that God gives us grace to step out, but His grace is activated by our faith. If we have failed, we must get back up and start walking again. There have been times when I woke up in the morning and could not seem to find contentment that day. I must get up and walk. Every day is a new day. Every day is a new battle. Your fight for truth will not be won once and for all. You must put on the shield of faith and pick up the sword of the Spirit and fight every day. Every day renew your mind to what is true. Every day put off the lies that Satan wants so desperately to use to deceive you. Every day, walk with your legacy in mind. Become what you want your heirs to be.

My exhortation to you is that which David spoke to his son Solomon in 1 Chronicles 28:10: *"Consider now, for the Lord has chosen you to build a temple as a sanctuary. Be strong and do the work"* (NIV). Now that is worth repeating: *"Be strong and do the work."* Be strong and fight the battle. In 2 Timothy, Paul exhorts his spiritual son to be strong, pass the legacy on, endure the tough times, keep himself free from the entanglement with the world, and strive to please God.

> *You therefore, my son, be strong in the grace that is in Christ Jesus. The things which you have heard from me in the presence of many witnesses, entrust these to faithful men who will be able to teach others also. Suffer hardship with me, as a good soldier of Christ Jesus. No soldier in active service entangles himself in the affairs of everyday life, so that he may please the one who enlisted him as a soldier.*
> —2 Timothy 2:1–4

Be strong not in your own strength, but in the grace that is Christ Jesus. Paul exhorted Timothy to be strong like a soldier because he knew he was in a battle. He was not in a physical battle, but a spiritual one. Ephesians 6:12 says, *"For our struggle is not against flesh and blood, but against the rulers, against the powers, against the world forces of this darkness, against the spiritual forces of wickedness in the heavenly places."* But God has not left you to fight the battle without weapons. He has provided full armor for us. We just have to put it on.

> *Therefore, take up the full armor of God, so that you will be able to resist in the evil day, and having done everything, to stand firm. Stand firm therefore, having girded your loins with truth, and having put on the breastplate of righteousness, and having shod your feet with the preparation of the gospel of peace; in addition to all, taking up the shield of faith with which you will be able to extinguish all the flaming arrows of the evil one. And take the helmet of salvation, and the sword of the Spirit, which is the word of God.*
> —Ephesians 6:13–17

The phrase *"stand firm"* denotes urgency. The breastplate of righteousness guards your heart from Satan's attacks. God has prepared you for the fight. Until the day that the clouds part and our Lord and Savior appears, we will have to get up and fight. Don't feel overwhelmed by Paul's exhortation. Fighting the battle does have its benefits:

> *It is a trustworthy statement: For if we died with Him, we will also live with Him; If we endure, we will also reign with Him; If we deny Him, He also will deny us; If we are faithless, He remains faithful, for He cannot deny Himself.*
> —2 Timothy 2:11–13

Paul tells us that if we endure, we will reign with Christ. But he also says that God is faithful even when we are faithless. There are days where I feel too weak to fight. There are days that I lose heart, but I am reminded of that trustworthy statement: God is faithful even when I am faithless (2 Timothy 2:13).

Your legacy will be echoed in the lives you influence—those who follow your lead, whether they are your physical children or spiritual offspring. These women will walk for a time in your shadow. Their lives will bear your marking. Anybody that knows me and my mother sees not only a physical similarity, but also a spiritual reflection of her in me. Jesus tells us that to whom much is given, much will be required. You have been given much, and God has given you the truth that will set you free. Be strong and courageous. Walk in that truth—walk in faith—walk in freedom.

As you begin to walk in freedom, God will give you increasing freedom with each step. With freedom comes responsibility. Paul states that we have the responsibility to test everything and hold on just to the good:

> *Test everything. Hold on to the good. Avoid every kind of evil. May God himself, the God of peace, sanctify you through and through. May your whole spirit, soul and body be kept blameless at the coming of our Lord Jesus Christ. The one who calls you is faithful and he will do it.*
> —1 Thessalonians 5:21–24 (NIV)

Test every thought and motive that comes your way. Is it from the Lord? Is it holy? Hold on to what is good. Then, Paul adds, we are to avoid evil. Some Bible translations say to abstain from evil. Avoid whatever causes you to stumble into sin. Avoid the scale in the bathroom. Avoid the magazines at the grocery store. Avoid the friends that feed your obsession. Then, the God of peace will make you holy—*"sanctify you through and through."* I pray that God will make you holy to the marrow of your bones. I pray that every breath you take will be one of freedom and truth. Finally, faithful is the One who calls you. Even when you feel as though you cannot take another step toward freedom, God is faithful to take the step with you.

May God's blessing of grace be poured out on your life. I pray that in the pages of this book, you have found freedom from being held captive to your body. May the eyes of your heart be enlightened to the falsehood that surrounds you. I hope that as you close this book, you will no longer allow falsehood to be your refuge, but that you will run to the truth and walk in the truth. You are chosen, holy, and beloved of God.

Body. Beauty. Boys.

Write your reactions to Sarah's thoughts in the conclusion. Which thoughts relate to you? Which ones don't relate to you? How did you feel as you read?

_____

_____

_____

_____

_____

_____

_____

_____

_____

_____

_____

_____

_____

_____

_____

_____

_____

New Hope® Publishers is a division of WMU®,
an international organization that challenges Christian believers
to understand and be radically involved in
God's mission. For more information about WMU,
go to www.wmu.com. More information
about New Hope books may be found at
www.newhopepublishers.com. New Hope books
may be purchased at your local bookstore.

More Great Books for Teens!

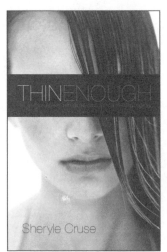

Thin Enough: My Spiritual Journey Through the Living Death of an Eating Disorder

Sheryle Cruse

Through faith and trust in God, teen girls can rise above the misery of eating disorders and enjoy promising futures.
1-59669-003-8

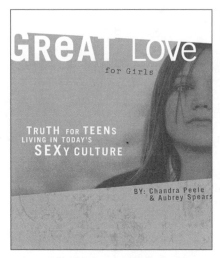

Great Love (for Girls): Truth for Teens in Today's Sexy Culture

Chandra Peele and Aubrey Spears

This candid four-week Bible study for teens presents a response to the world's distorted view of sexuality.
1-56309-964-0

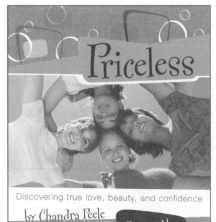

Priceless: Discovering True Love, Beauty, and Confidence

Chandra Peele

This six-week interactive Bible study helps teen girls know that they are priceless.
1-56309-909-8

A Girl's Life With God

Casey Hartley Gibbons

A former Miss American Teen encourages girls to grow in Christ now and not wait until adulthood to make a difference in the world.
1-56309-757-5

new
hope
PUBLISHERS